Photography produced by Kasey Lane Photography at: https://www.facebook.com/KaseyLanePhotography

Cover design by Racmad Agus - Racdesign Concept

Requests to the Publisher for permission should be addressed online at ModernSamuraiSociety.com

For general information on other products and services, please contact us online at the ModernSamuraiSociety.com

To get bulk copies of this book, please contact us online at ModernSamurai-Society.com.

Published by:

Writers Rise

Kelowna, British Columbia

Web: writersrise.com

Dedication

This book is dedicated to all those who answer the call to train in the martial arts. To the young and old, experienced and novice. To those who show up for training consistently. To those who persevere past the pain, past the defeats and, most of all, past the ego. This book is for you.

Acknowledgement

An old samurai tale speaks of a young samurai in search of a Zen master who could help him understand the workings of his own mind. It was customary for samurai to seek the teachings of a master to help improve his skills and live a life of honor.

The young samurai found an old master living in the countryside. He bowed to the master and asked, "Please teach me the ways of heaven and hell."

But the Zen master looked at him up and down and exclaimed, "Me? Teach you the ways of heaven and hell? Why, look at the way your belly jiggles! You must be fooling around, young man!"

The young samurai turned pink with embarrassment, which quickly grew into a fiery red rage. He brandished his sword, ready to attack the Zen master. But the wise old man stood calmly and said, "That is hell."

The young samurai, realizing his lesson, bowed in gratitude. The Zen master said, "That is heaven."

As modern samurai, we strive to experience the heaven that is the constant realization and acknowledgement of the good things that happen to us. I am deeply thankful to have been given the opportunity to share the wisdom I have gained in my training, but I am even more indebted to the people who have made this possible.

To my friend and photographer, **Kasey Van Sickle**. You deserve more than a mention in the Acknowledgment page. Both you and I know that, without you, this book would not be here at all.

To **Sean McHugh** and **Team First Strike** (a great place to train), for allowing the use of your facilities for the photographs in this book. And to **Kyle Van Sickle**'s Muay Thai class and the use of his students, as well as Jamie Wooton and his MMA class.

From **Beverly Dick**, my very first martial instructor, to **Dr. Serge LaFlamme**, my current Chief Instructor. Thank you for dedicating your lives to passing down your knowledge and passion for the martial arts. There are many instructors and training partners along the way have helped me that I can't possibly name them all.

Just a few of these training partners include, **Don Seel**, **Scott Schaffrick**, **Cory Singleton**, **Heinz Schlief**, **Tony Williamson**, **Todd Ueda**, **Matt McNally**, **Nick Austin** and **Darren Bockman**. There are more...

To **Marian Mauler aka Muggsy** and **Dariel Vogel**, my yoga instructors from Narramata and Okanagan Falls. Thank you for your wisdom and patience in teaching me to balance body and mind and bring peace and harmony to balance the harsher techniques of martial training.

To **Nick Brodd** of nickbrodd.com, my partner at Writers Rise, for introducing the concept of myelin to me and showing me how muscle memory works, and for allowing me to share his information with my readers.

And to all the Masters who dedicated their lives to honing the greatest skill and martial knowledge and then passing it on to others. Without the Masters of the past, I would not be here at all.

And also, to **Nicole Arce** for your insightful editing, and to **Rachmad Agus** for a great cover design.

This modern samurai bows in gratitude.

Table of Contents

Preface

Statistically, violent confrontation occurs at a greater rate during times of prohibition and downturns in the economy. We are living in those times and the chances that someone wants you to be their next victim in this lifetime are high.

You may feel compelled to read about self-defense, which is why you picked up this book. The consequences of being unprepared in dealing with violence and brutality aimed at you or your family are dire and deadly. You will find many books written about martial arts. A great many books have been written on the how-to aspect of martial arts, which teach you how to warm up, how to perform basic techniques, etc. I look through my personal library of martial arts literature and around 90% of them contain explanations and accompanying pictures that demonstrate how to perform the basic kicking, punching and grappling moves. They show pictures of smiling practitioners, sitting down, stretching or in a push-up position. The remaining 10% of these books deal with the aspect of mental preparation for tournament fighting. They talk about meditation and achieving one with your training.

While these are all fantastic for the beginner, the vast majority of them are simply what someone else has already written while incorporating their own personal spin on it. Where I feel an improvement opportunity lies is in dissecting that moment when you are attacked. We want to break it down and understand what happens to you during that very moment—why your pulse rises and you lose your fine motor skills and how to inoculate yourself from the stress of the situation. It is my intent to deal with the heart of the matter. The primary focus of self-defense and the martial arts should be dealing with confrontation.

Confrontation exists whenever some form of disagreement, conflict, disappointment or unwanted aggression aligns itself squarely with YOU. It may happen in a flash or may have a slow build-up, which allows you to employ appropriate avoidance measures. It is a natural instinct to avoid confrontation. Certainly, there is no shame in walking away. In the animal kingdom, when male lions or bears stand off, there is usually a lot of grandstanding. They growl and roar and puff up, but neither one of them really wants an all-out battle. The wild beast knows that confrontation can injure it. Complications from this injury can prevent the animal from getting food, which leads to its starvation and eventual death.

Like the lion or the bear that backs off, the skilled black belt should have the personal confidence to walk away from a situation without affecting his or her ego.

The chances that you will experience a violent encounter are real. We know this. This is why we train. This is why we seek knowledge to prepare ourselves physically and mentally so that we can protect ourselves and our family. Despite the numerous books on the subject of self-defense and martial arts, there seems to be meager coverage on one of the most important elements: the mental preparation to cope with an unreasonable person's brutality.

Put yourself in the shoes of an attacker who would impose his will upon you. Visualize the outcome he envisions. What do you see? That would be you, lying on the ground, broken and bloody and perhaps the victim of a dominated sexual attack. This image evokes powerful emotion in me as it should to you. Take the appropriate measure to protect yourself from the stress of the situation and give yourself the upper hand. Simply having the mindset of not being a willing victim goes a long way in preventing a violent violation. If I have done my job properly, by the end of this book, you will be better equipped to crush the confrontation.

How to Use this Book

This book is a collection of lessons that span a wide variety of topics, including but not limited to: situational awareness, self-defense, achieving your black belt, defending yourself and your family, the changes in your body during a physical confrontation and, more importantly, how to use all this knowledge to your advantage. You will also encounter lesser known methods of self-defense, developing killer instinct and the occasional scenario training.

Because of the sporadic and sometimes random nature of the lessons I have learned throughout my martial and security-related endeavors, the topics in this book may first appear to have a random order. You should be able to pick up the book and open the pages to one of the brief chapters and hopefully walk away with a bit more martial knowledge than you had before.

Throughout this book, I will refer to strategy and tactics. When I mention strategy, I refer to your overall approach to training. When I refer to tactics, I am talking about the moment-to-moment moves you execute to achieve a specific goal.

My ultimate goal in writing this book is to pass on knowledge that my amazing instructors have passed on to me. If even just one student in the martial arts or any person who does not have a calling to train benefits from this knowledge by avoiding a dangerous situation for themselves or their family, all the time and effort put into recording these lessons have not been wasted.

Introduction

It was late into the year 1983. Fall registration for Dick's School of Karate in Hinton, Alberta was underway. I was only 11 years old but I already had my fair share of fights both on the school ground and off. I was there only because of one thing: I wanted to learn to fight better. I wanted to be able to take on multiple opponents. I wanted to never worry about someone mugging me with a wrench again.

Before moving to Hinton, my father had found business opportunities in Fort McMurray in northern Alberta. I was in grade two at that time. We lived on the first floor of an apartment building where I had a friend on the top floor. One day, as I was walking down the stairs after visiting my friend on the uppermost floor, with a yummy orange Popsicle in hand, I met a large boy blocking my way to the first floor. He held a pipe wrench in his hand and glanced lustfully at the orange Popsicle I had just unwrapped.

I still remember clearly to this day how he demanded that I give him half my treat. Waving the pipe wrench in front of me, he said, "You give me half of that Popsicle or I'm going to hit you in the head with this wrench." Remember, I was only a small kid in grade two back then. My mugger was many years older than me and was a lot bigger. With shaking hands, I hit the Popsicle on the railing and it snapped neatly in half. I quickly handed him what he demanded and ran home.

And so, walking into my very first martial arts class, I still had the picture of the big kid waving his pipe wrench at me. My heart beat loudly against my chest. It was a small karate club in a small town. There were no kids' classes. At eleven years old, I trained with the adults.

The instructor carried a special message for us younger students: "I know every one of your teachers. If you use what I'm going to teach you to fight in school, it will not be the teachers you have to worry about."

I was adamant. I was here because I wanted to fight better. I thought to myself that I could probably avoid fighting for six months. During that time, I would learn everything I need to know about martial arts. Then if I get kicked out of the club after that, so what? Such was my mindset at the time. It amuses me to think back on those days and remember my actual reason for starting training in martial arts.

Fast-forward 30 years later, here I am reflecting back upon almost an entire lifetime of training in one style or aspect of martial arts or another. The number of ways that martial training has aided and enhanced my life is far beyond the scope of this book.

Having worked as a bouncer in a bar and in event security for many years, I have been in countless altercations. I have been jumped from behind, and I have successfully dealt with two people attacking me at once. It seems my initial childhood dream has come true. All that time, I lost only one fight. The lessons that I learned from my victories and defeats along with the countless lessons from the partners and amazing instructors that I have had will unfold in the pages that follow.

"It is not the critic who counts; not the man who points out how the strong man stumbles, or where the doer of deeds could have done them better. The credit belongs to the man who is actually in the arena, whose face is marred by dust and sweat and blood; who strives valiantly; who errs, who comes short again and again, because there is no effort without error and shortcoming; but who does actually strive to do the deeds; who knows great enthusiasms, the great devotions; who spends himself in a worthy cause; who at the best knows in the end the triumph of high achievement, and who at the worst, if he fails, at least fails while daring greatly, so that his place shall never be with those cold and timid souls who neither know victory nor defeat."

Theodore Roosevelt, *The Man In the Arena*

Chapter 1
The Devolving Nature of Conflict

Not too long ago, one man could challenge another to a fight. There would be an almost unspoken set of rules that the two would adhere to. Call it a code of honor. This is clearly not the case anymore, far from it.

Violence is everywhere. It has increasingly turned nasty and random. You can become a victim of assault anytime, anywhere. You can no longer count on one party to a fight, ceasing the attack once the other participant was rendered defenseless. Ju-Jitsu and martial arts similar to it used to be considered harsh and barely within the law. But because of the increasing brutality of violence, Ju-Jitsu and other similar arts are not only the appropriate response, it is the preferred response. The art you choose to practice must adapt with the times.

Back in the day, a man would get knocked to the ground and that was the end of it. Fighters lived up to their code of honor. These days, whether it is through a decline in social values, children being raised by the television because of parents working one-and-a-half jobs, or the deteriorating economic conditions we are living in, the nature of violence has taken a nasty turn. One needs only turn on the news to discover evidence of literally insane acts of violence that were previously unheard of. You hear about levels of aggression that can only be described as vicious as they are reported in all their gory detail.

Your style of self-defense needs to adapt with the times. It must address all possible ranges of combat. One style that is not only considered entirely appropriate but is actually preferred by many law enforcement bodies, bodyguard agencies and individual security license holders is Ju-Jitsu. It fits the bill perfectly. There are many styles of Ju-Jitsu, and not all of them adapt with the times. The progressive styles of Ju-Jitsu that adapt to the changing societal norms are the styles of choice. Of course, there are many styles of martial arts that will work to shore up your defenses against violent aggression. By the end of this book, we will have adequately explored this topic.

As the nature of violence continues to change, so should your chosen art and the rules of engagement that are taught to students. Please commit to memory the laws of your land. Understand that the definition of excessive force is force that is applied after it is no longer necessary to continue to apply that force. Always train with the mindset of 100% commitment to your defense once you are forced into action, but know where the lines exist. Discuss with fellow students scenarios where someone was goaded into a fight. Could they have walked away? Could they have talked their way out of it? Having regular discussions like this sharpens your decision-making skills and helps you decide whether you must fight to defend yourself or walk away. These skills are invaluable.

Because of the increasing senselessness and randomness of violence, your art of choice must reflect the changing nature of violence in our society today. It must adapt in order to provide you, the student, with the most practical, effective tools at your disposal. If morals and economic times continue to erode, I suspect the self-defense styles of tomorrow will increase their levels of harshness to manage the threats of the day.

Chapter 2
The Most Important Self-Defense Skill

You are on this martial path because you realize that you cannot count on anyone else to look after you. You have taken responsibility for this task yourself. You refuse to be like the vast majority who wander around with their head in the clouds, the ones who meander about in a haze of unawareness. It is the skill of awareness that we need to develop.

You know that the governmental system is in place to protect you only after the problem has occurred. The fire department shows up after the fire is set ablaze only to put out the fire. The police show up after the assault has taken place only to track down your violators. This is simply not good enough for you .You are building a sense of situational awareness that will provide you with the huge benefit of being alerted to danger before it happens, allowing you to avoid the confrontation in the first place.

There are a wide variety of skill sets that you want to possess, skills like swimming, first aid, and of course, self-defense. All of this allows you to take care of yourself much more efficiently. It allows you to become more self-reliant instead of waiting for others to come to your aid. You recognize this responsibility lies on your shoulders and your shoulders alone. This means being physically equipped with the right skill sets and being mentally prepared to deal with the things that may confront you.

What this all boils down to is the idea of recognizing the dangers around you and being prepared for them. In order to do this, you must see the world through a different set of eyes, the eyes of awareness. I don't like the word "paranoia", but an interesting exercise is to develop an almost artificial paranoia, for a brief time, wondering to yourself what danger could lurk around every corner.

It's like being a driver with a perfect driving record. More often than not, when you ask all the good drivers out there how they're able to maintain such a clean record with all the bad drivers out there, they all have a similar habit. They imagine what bad things could happen and quickly plan out how to avoid the potential danger. That driver up ahead, what if they turned into my lane without warning? So they check the lanes beside them to determine which lane they could swerve into if that happens. This requires them to be aware of their surroundings at all times. And so it is with self-defense.

Say hello to the three A's.

Awareness.
Be completely aware of your surroundings.
Anticipation.
Anticipate the problems that you may encounter. Formulate quick plans ahead of time when you anticipate these potential problems.
Avoidance.
This is self-explanatory. Awareness and anticipation provide for you the ability to avoid most problems.

Throughout the following chapters, the triple theme of awareness, anticipation and avoidance will reveal itself both in training suggestions and stories told where the lesson was learned the hard way and passed to you here in this book that you hold in your hand.

That the average mugger or attacker is looking for easy victims, combined with the above strategy, will ensure you will avoid most trouble. Adopt the mindset of awareness, anticipation and avoidance.

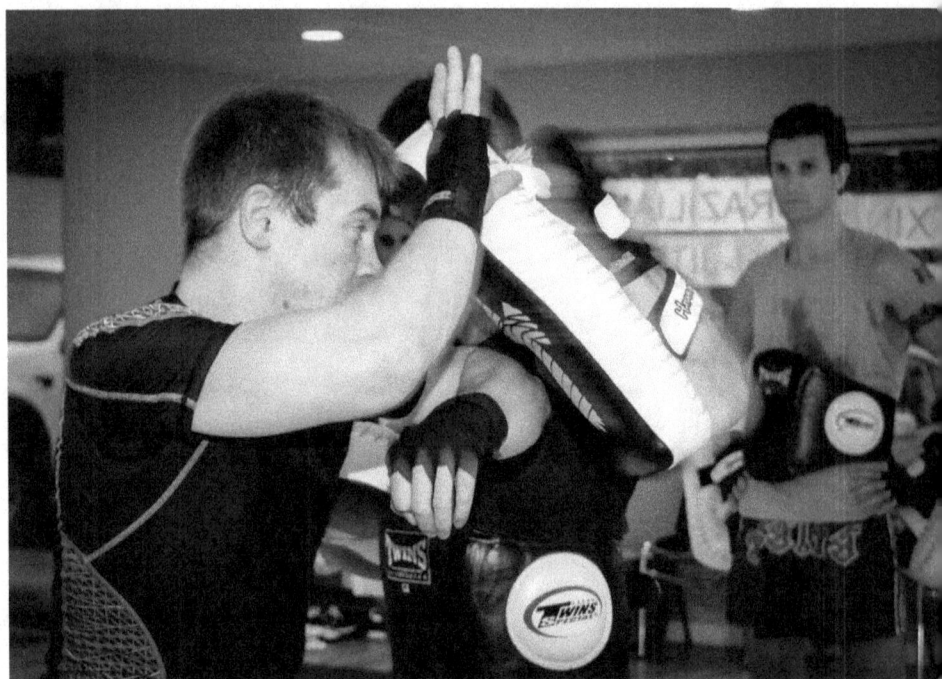

Chapter 3
Self-Defense, You Say?

Are you and interested in self-defense information? Any person who is serious about self-defense training or learning how to protect themselves and their family must acquaint themselves with the laws of his land.

Self-defense is more than just learning to block, parry and punch. It means learning to protect yourself from any situation that can cause you or your family harm.

If you were forced to defend yourself and your attacker was seriously injured or happened to die and you found yourself in jail, this would definitely be a situation that you would need to defend yourself against. How can you provide for your family if you are incarcerated? How will you defend yourself against the hardened criminals you may encounter in jail? How will you defend yourself against that laundry room prison gang rape?

I am using hyperbole, of course, but you get my point. Self-defense means avoiding trouble in the first place. If you are forced to use your skills to defend yourself, you do so with the least worry or probability that you'll end up on the wrong side of the law as a result.

How do you accomplish this? You need to know the laws of your land and how they are applied. Remember, I am not a lawyer, and I'm not offering legal advice but I will provide you with the basic rules.

If you are also Canadian, you will want to know the following:

"Everyone who is assaulted without having provoked the assault is justified in repelling force by force if the force he uses is not intended to cause death or grievous bodily harm and is no more than necessary to enable him to defend himself."

The critical point here is using "reasonable force" under the circumstances you found yourself in.

"If you do cause death or grievous bodily harm, you are justified if you use the force under reasonable apprehension of death or grievous bodily harm."

If you genuinely believed that your attacker was going to harm or kill you and you harmed or killed them in the process of defending yourself, you may be justified if a judge or jury would have acted in the same manner if they found themselves in the same circumstances that you found yourself in.

For the purposes of self-defense, provocation includes words, blows or gestures.

Words - verbal threats of harm towards you that you believe are real

Blows - actual physical contact in an aggressive manner

Gestures - motions for actions towards you indicating intended harm

The purpose of this information is to give you generally accepted justification for initiating your self-defense. Obviously, the threat you acted against must have been perceived as real and an average person under similar circumstances would have believed the same.

"Everyone who is lawfully using force is criminally responsible for any excess thereof according to the nature and quality of the act that constitutes the excess."

What this means is that if you use more force than a reasonable person would have under similar circumstances, you can be held liable for your actions.

Do not allow yourself to fall into some legal quagmire. Learn the laws of your land and how they are applied. Commit these rules of engagement to memory and climb the ranks of the modern samurai. Again, consult a lawyer if you aren't clear with how the laws you'll be judged by are applied.

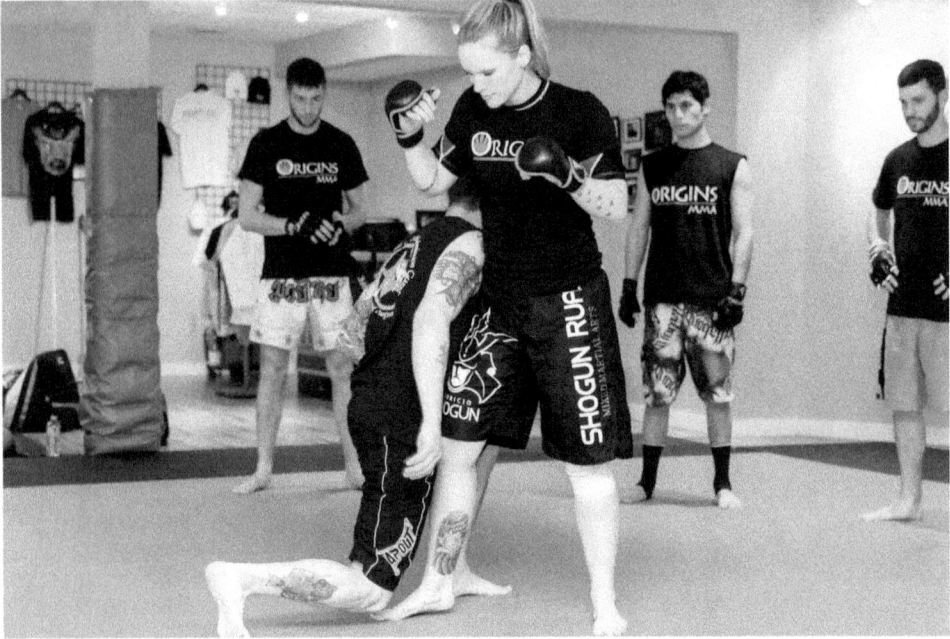

Chapter 4
Victim Mind

Every morning in Africa, a gazelle wakes up. It knows it must outrun the fastest lion or it will be killed. Every morning in Africa, a lion wakes up. It knows it must run faster than the slowest gazelle or it will starve. It doesn't matter whether you're the lion or a gazelle—when the sun comes up, you'd better be running."
— Christopher McDougall

We are mammals, a product of evolution. As such, we can learn a lot about our primal instincts by observing other animals in their natural habitat. How do they treat each other? How do predators select their prey? Much can be gleaned from observing nature to dig inside the mindset of the predator, find out what he is looking for and make sure that we are not it. More importantly, we can find out what the predator doesn't want to see and adapt those qualities into our personal makeup. This act of shoring up goes a long way towards preventing yourself from becoming a victim.

Have you ever watched a nature program where some poor gazelle or some other unfortunate animal is turned into a meal by a lion or some other unforgiving predator? Did you feel sorry for the victim? Did you look away during the animal's last breaths, during the final death blow? I have. You can learn a lot by watching these terrible demonstrations of raw nature. There are predators, and there are prey.

The predator always selects the weak, slow or injured and dying, a meal of opportunity. And so, too, like the lion skulking in the grasses of the savannah, the human predator watches from the corner of the bar for that individual who is overly intoxicated and alone, paying a large bill in cash and preparing to walk home alone. The human predator seeks out the weak. He seeks out the meek. And the weaker you appear, the more likely you become a victim. Always remember that the violent criminal, when in need for his next "fix" or whatever the hell he wants, looks for easy targets without fail.

The last thing the human predator is looking for is confrontation. He's counting on an easy win, an easy victory. He is not looking for a fight. If you make it absolutely clear right from the beginning that, regardless of where the situation goes, you will fight for your life, will inflict at least some damage and will not go quietly into the night, the predator will move on. The predator will look for an easier target.

Are you a predator or are you prey?

Do not get the wrong impression. I advocate against puffing your chest out and being cocky. I am not suggesting you become a predator. You've learned from nature and understand the hierarchy. Know that, when attacked, you will turn on your inner Alpha male (or female) and fight back, defend yourself and your family with ferocious violence and intense brutality. This is simply a part of your mental makeup. It is evident in your confidence. It is evident in how you carry yourself. While conducting your business today, observe the people around you. Do they throw off the vibe of predator or prey? More importantly, which one are you?

Chapter 5
The Appropriate Answer

Imagine yourself waiting for the subway. A stranger taps you on the shoulder to ask directions. Would you react with your set of devastating techniques and incapacitate the stranger in one-and-a-half seconds? Of course you wouldn't. That would be inappropriate.

At the same time, if you found yourself in a scenario with multiple attackers or someone attempting to stab you with a knife; it would be just as misguided to employ gentle tactics. Your response must be appropriate to match the threat presented to you.

With this in mind, you must train a system of self-defense that instills tactics and techniques with a complete range of options that you can draw upon during your time of need. Techniques taught should include:

- Heavy impact striking with all of your body's "weapons" to appropriate, vulnerable areas
- Holds/locks and joint manipulation or control tactics
- Throwing/clinch/CQB and takedowns
- Grappling
- Common weapons familiarization up to complete proficiency
- Verbal Ju-Jitsu or preplanned confrontation avoidance strategies

Individually the above techniques have their own limitations and their merits but when trained holistically, they can combine to form a complete system of practical, effective self-defense. This complete system will allow the student or practitioner to respond appropriately to the level of threat he happens to find himself mired in. This is the kind of self-defense system you want to spend your time with.

Systems of self-defense that do not embrace the above are not able to give the practitioner all options available. Incomplete styles or systems hinder the ability to respond appropriately. This doesn't mean that you must quit the system you currently train simply because it doesn't incorporate stick fighting in it, for instance. What it does necessitate is an awareness that your overall strategy may need some shoring up in places.

It is not my intention to put any one style of martial arts down, not at all. Just keep in mind that not all martial arts systems are a good fit if personal protection or self-defense is your primary concern. Some of the earlier systems of martial arts that I participated in claimed to instill in their students "excellent" self-defense skills, while at the same time teaching the student to stand in front of their attacker with their fists on their hips. This always baffled me, as I never saw a boxer in front of a fresh opponent with his hands down. Please do not take this as a slight to styles that maintain tradition. They have their place and will be covered in an upcoming passage.

If self-defense or making it home in relatively good condition after being attacked is your primary concern, then training to choose the correct response is how you want to spend your time. It just makes sense to use as straight a line as possible to defending yourself.

This correct response we keep referring to is a skill that can be and should be learned. Through consistent practice, both through physical training and your scenario training, as well as talk-through philosophical discussions on when it is necessary to drop the hammer, reinforcement of what is appropriate becomes automatic. It becomes second nature.

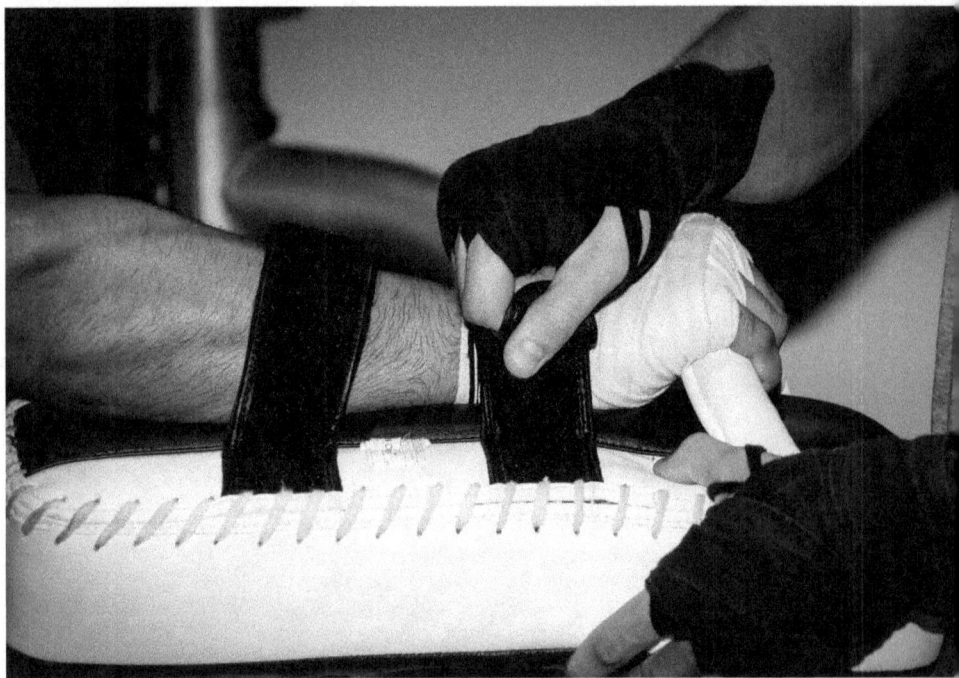

Chapter 6

Self-Defense,
Not Self-Defeat

"But I didn't hit him full force."

Have you ever heard someone make this seemingly ridiculous claim? There's this idea that a technique, or yourself for that matter, has a volume dial which you can use to adjust how much force you can apply. The concept that you will apply only 80% or 50% of your full force when you are going to strike someone is a misguided one.

When faced with a potentially violent confrontation, your training should provide you with instant recognition as to which response is required to stop the threat and prevent it from existing further. When faced with any given threat, your choice is to choose which response is appropriate to match the level of threat presented, not in how hard you choose to hit.

Never be of the mindset that you could use the same technique you would for a very serious situation on a less serious situation and only use it at half force, as if the threat presented was only half-serious.

Think of a golfer on the golf course. After a certain level of experience or training, the golfer will know with fair accuracy how far away he is from the hole and which corresponding club to use. If he is close to the hole, he's not going to pull out a big club like a driver and use it at only half force. This would be ridiculous. He would not be very effective in achieving his desired outcome. (Thanks, Dad, for the golf training.)

And so it is with self-defense. You choose the appropriate response and, once you have chosen, you dedicate yourself 100% to that response. If you find that in the middle of the self-defense technique you are using, the attacker is no longer able to continue to attack you, you simply stop. I have a series of techniques that I use when I'm attacked abruptly or suddenly. And not once have I been able to make it to the end of that string of techniques. The attacker has always crumbled defenseless in the middle of that set of techniques. At that point, I stop.

You practice until you achieve the point where you can determine which response is appropriate for the given situation. Once decided, you commit 100% to your response. When that golfer is really close to the green, he uses his wedge. But he still uses that wedge with 100% commitment. So too shall you use the correct technique with 100% commitment.

Imagine only hitting your opponent half hard. What may result? He may lose respect for your ability. He may double his efforts in attacking. He may notice you have some self-defense training and may now even choose to use his harshest techniques or perhaps a weapon that you haven't noticed before.

It never serves you to hit half hard. Trust your training. It will instill in you the instinct to choose the appropriate response. And once you have chosen, give 100% commitment to the course of action until that action is no longer required.

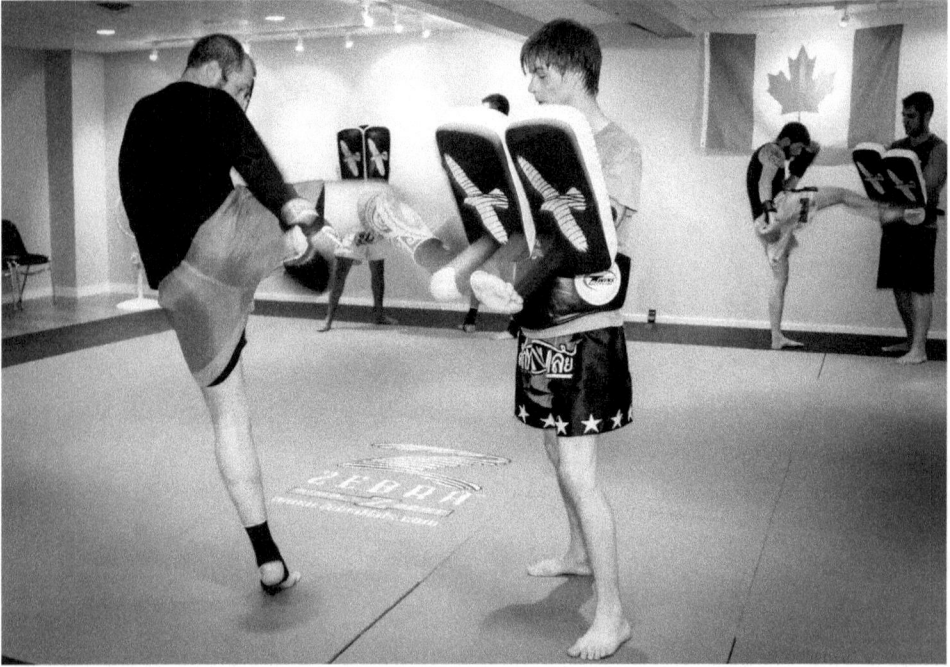

Chapter 7
Do You Have a
Global Approach?

Self-defense or physical confrontation begins with some form of threat, whether it is a real or perceived threat. It ends when that threat no longer exists. It doesn't matter how serious the threat is. If it affects or is about to affect your life, it requires that you pay attention to your self-defense strategy, your overall approach to self-defense.

Here begins the distinction between individual techniques and your overall strategy. Think of it as strategy vs. tactics. Your strategy is your overall approach. Your tactics are the moment-to-moment individual techniques that you would choose.

Your whole defense to any given threat may involve many individual techniques strung together with the purpose of stopping the threat and removing it from existence. Individual techniques can be easy to learn on their own, but your global defense strategy is one that you put together after practice, time and experience. Your global strategy instructs you how to use these individual techniques and how to apply them appropriately to threat situations so that you choose which techniques to use for whatever threat happens to be at hand.

Think of self-defense in terms of the whole approach, your global strategy. When the average person thinks of self-defense, he may imagine a physical technique, like blocking a punch that is swung at his face. Self-defense is much more than that. It is a global approach—comprehensive, all-inclusive.

Most people aren't aware that keeping your car in good working order or keeping up your health and maintaining physical fitness are self-defense. These things are absolutely self-defense. Even keeping your financial affairs in reasonable shape is self-defense because becoming mired in debt can cause chronic stress that can lead to serious health problems. Self-defense is all about preventing and then protecting you from problems. It is protecting yourself and your family from beginning to end. Your overall plan of self-defense is something that begins when you wake up in the morning but doesn't end when you go to sleep.

Approach your training with your whole attention and know what piece of the puzzle you are training today. Are you picking out one tactic and putting the high polish of repetition to it so that when it is inserted back into the string of techniques, the overall quality has improved? Or are you training more of a strategic angle, like the movement drills of a multiple-attackers scenario where the overall goal is not allowing yourself to be surrounded?

While individual techniques, like strikes or parrying techniques, can be learned rather easily, it takes experience and practice to learn how to put them together in a practical and effective manner. Be consistent with your training and keep the training purpose in mind. You will attain your global self-defense goals.

Chapter 8

What If You Did Nothing?

You're in an all-night Laundromat. Although you rarely find yourself in places like these at 2:00 AM, here you are. While you're folding your laundry, you are startled when someone bursts through the door. A man in his late twenties rushes past you with a frantic and terrified look. He goes to the back of the Laundromat and crouches down behind one of the dryers. Without much delay, the door bursts open again. This time, there are two larger men with intense looks on their faces. One moves to the front while the other heads to the back of the room where the frightened man is hiding. The man closest to the dryer yells, "James, he's over here!" In no time, the two men corner the frightened man and close in on him. It is obvious that something serious is about to happen. What do you do?

I used to have a martial arts instructor who would begin most classes with some form of discussion or lecture. Sometimes the discussions would pertain to the required knowledge needed to advance in the ranks. Other times, self-defense scenarios such as the one above would be played out or discussed among the students. The man had an amazing ability to get you thinking about confrontational scenarios, deciding when to act and, more importantly, how to deal with confrontation in an intelligent manner. It is making these decisions ahead of time that really helps the student develop his own personalized **rules of engagement** when facing confrontation.

When faced with the above scenario, the average student would instinctively respond with a reply like, "I would rush over there and stand beside the man about to be attacked. Two on one isn't fair, and he clearly needs some help. I don't want to see an innocent man getting the daylights pounded out of him right in front of me. I am a black belt, after all."

Of course, this response would seem the right and noble thing to do. After all, he trains martial arts for a reason right? Is it not a virtuous act to help the weaker, outnumbered individual?

Then you learn that the frightened man is scared for a reason. He just finished raping James' sister and he's done it before. Are you going to help a rapist? Perhaps the man is a violent escaped convict and the pursuers are undercover police officers. The student would always be shocked and backpedaling with his speech. Of course, he doesn't want to help the rapist or convict, but his moral fiber would not allow him to stand idly by and watch this horror unfold while he was capable of doing something. Yes, we are capable of doing something, which is what makes us want to act. But what is the appropriate response?

Appropriate Response

You are rarely in possession of all of the facts, so find out. But don't take one side over the other without knowing more about the situation. If you feel you must become involved, you have to turn it into a self-defense situation. You cannot jump in, grab somebody and start hitting him because you think he's doing wrong. How the hell do you know? You must turn it into a self-defense situation. How do you do that? You can start off by yelling, "Stop!" Then immediately say, "Now look, I don't want any trouble but what is going on here?" You assert yourself with your open hands up, palms facing the situation. You're certainly not holding fists. Open hands, please. From that point, you can attempt to get more information before you act hastily but you have made it abundantly clear that you don't want any trouble.

Chapter 9
The Power of Calm

Confrontation is naturally an emotionally charged event. The untrained individual allows himself to be easily drawn into the realm of over-aggressiveness or that machismo-fueled puffing up, like a peacock or some other grandstanding animal. Leave this display for the amateurs. It does not help you. We believe in avoiding confrontation whenever possible. This is our primary goal. As such, when faced with an aggressor, we neither agitate nor challenge him. At the same time, we certainly do not present ourselves as meek or some effortlessly dominated target ready for easy pickings.

It astonishes me how some people are so easily manipulated. When you find yourself in a situation that gets your blood boiling and you feel compelled to react like some sort of animal, take a moment to consider how you plan to respond. What will your response mean? Consider the following scenario.

You've been waiting for a parking spot patiently with your indicating signals on. All of the sudden, a rude person snatches your spot! You were there first. You clearly had your intentions signaled but the other person was thinking only of himself. He stole your spot. Recognize that you do have the ability to choose your response here. This may seem obvious to most, but many people out there still need to heed the lesson. Merely reacting is allowing yourself and, in essence, a part of your life to be manipulated or controlled to some degree by someone else. This is not acceptable to the forward-thinking martial artist.

The best revenge is living well.

I love YouTube. You can watch so many confrontations posted not only for your amusement but for educational purposes as well. How many times have you watched a fight about to happen, where an aggressor is taunting and using words to goad another person into a fight? Perhaps he is attempting to get the other person to throw the first punch. What if the other man stood there and remained calm? Wouldn't this confound the aggressor? Would this not rattle his sense of dominance?

Remember that the aggressor is the unnatural one here. Don't take his bullshit personally. Do not absorb his aggressiveness. Of course, aggressiveness has its place in confrontational situations, but why alert your potential attacker to your mindset? Remain calm and give him nothing. Give him neutrality. Stick to your game plan, remain neutral and remove yourself from the situation as soon as possible. Remember that our primary directive is one of avoiding trouble in the first place.

Chapter 10
Now It's My Turn

What is your underlying strategy when faced with an unreasonable person who insists on imposing his will upon you? What is your foundational belief system for situations like this? A martial arts practitioner who is truly interested in the most practical and effective forms of self-defense must subscribe to the idea that when an aggressor initiates some form of attack, that first point of contact, that attack, should be the very last chance he gets to initiate any other action during your exchange.

There is something that occurs, some form of action on the part of the aggressor, that causes you to pull the trigger. There is something in his mannerisms and actions that tell you to respond. If you have worked in the security industry or have been around physical confrontation more than a few times, you begin to recognize when a physical confrontation is inevitable.

But you never want to feel as though you know exactly what is going to happen. Always leave room for the unexpected. In other words, never become complacent. Always keep some form of guard up or enough of a reactionary gap to avoid being caught off guard.

Getting back to the point, the moment that trigger is pulled is when you must seize control of the situation. It's a mistake to be continually reacting to your opponent's offensive initiatives. If this is your game plan, then you are continually left at his mercy, continually reacting. When I was a teenager and involved in my first traditional martial art, Kempo karate, I experienced this many times while sparring. I would find myself in the ring and the ref would yell "Kumute!" And there I was, almost overwhelmed by continually bobbing, weaving, blocking and backpedaling. In my defense, I was always sparring against more experienced students, always sparring against higher belts. I had yet to learn this valuable lesson.

Have you ever heard this? "I don't believe in violence, I don't believe in harming another human being no matter what their actions are." The idea of not wanting to harm your aggressor is nice to some. I suppose it could be achieved if you are either fighting a weak child or you had already devoted a large portion of your life to martial training to develop enough skill and expertise to be able to redirect and parry a larger, stronger opponent until he got tired and gave up trying to hurt you.

Please do not misunderstand my point. It is great to have the attitude of "Do no harm", but when a person puts or attempts to put their hands, or any other body part for that matter, on you, with the intent to cause harm, you not only have the right to defend yourself, you MUST stop that action NOW. Take the initiative away from your opponent, and never let him re-establish his composure during the balance of the event.

Chapter 11
Who Threw the First Punch?

How many times have you heard this? Maybe it brings back images of standing in the schoolyard with lots of kids walking around aggressively with the teacher trying to figure out "who was at fault." As if the person that threw the first punch was always automatically the one to blame for the fight. It's an interesting idea and I suppose that most of the time it's true. After all, sticks and stones may break my bones, but names will never hurt me, right?

This is almost always great advice for kids when they are learning how to behave in the real world. You don't want to raise children believing the idea of hitting first and asking questions later. But in the reality in which we live, this is not always true.

The person who throws the first blow in a fight, more often than not, is the victor. How is it acceptable that when you are doing everything you can to avoid a fight you must let this jerk in front of you actually lay his hands on you before you are morally or legally released into action? I call bullshit. There are times when it makes perfect sense to initiate your self-defense.

The aggressor in an altercation is the one who presses the action, the one who will not allow you to walk away. It is not simply a matter of who strikes first. If any reasonable person in your shoes would decide that an attack is imminent, you are justified in striking first. You may even gain a psychological advantage by initiating your self-defense. Your initiation could end the confrontation right then and there with your first move. The overall magnitude or amount of violence can be reduced to just your opening move. And, of course, you will not simply be reacting to your opponent's attacks if you seize the initiative once a confrontation is certain.

It is simply ridiculous when two men face off and are about to fight. They push or shove on each other's chests several times before one decides to throw the first punch, it usually being a right haymaker to the face. Whenever you see this, you have to suspect that the participants know nothing of self-defense or the martial arts. The moment someone gets within your personal space and you allow them the ability to put their hands on you, you are at an extreme disadvantage. The guys who are about to fight and puff their chests up and bump them with the other person, they are so close to each other that whoever strikes first will probably hit the other person. And if he capitalizes on that momentum, he will win the fight.

The point is simple. You have tried everything reasonable to avoid this confrontation. When it is abundantly clear that you cannot walk away or talk your way out of it, that is the moment to pull the trigger. That is the moment to seize the opportunity to stop the imminent threat and prevent it from continuing.

Note: I am not a lawyer, and am not offering legal advice. Know the laws of your land and how they pertain to self-defense. Consult a lawyer and take his or her advice.

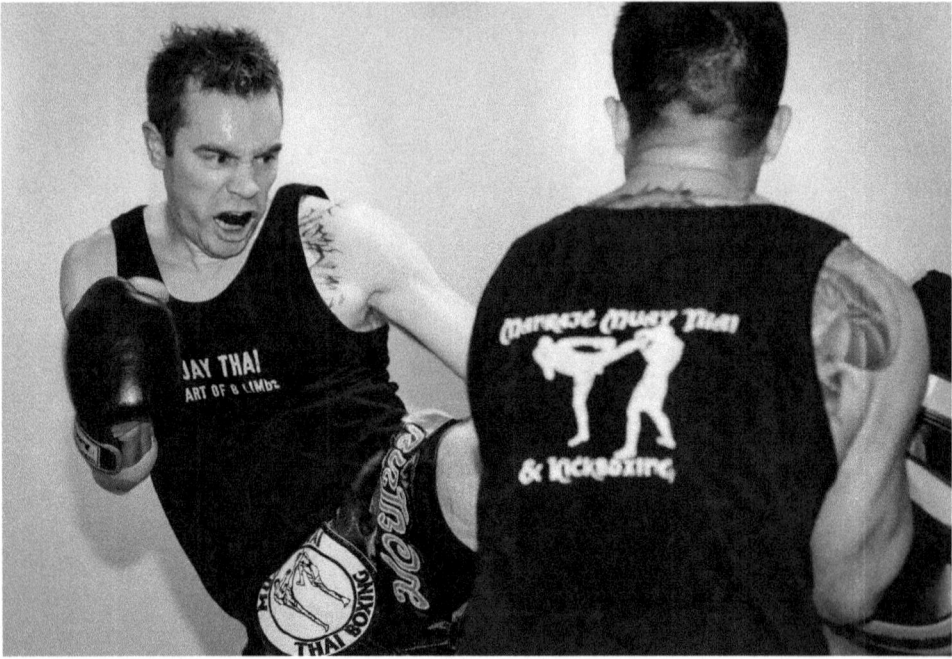

Chapter 12

The Critical Truth

The most important piece of your physical self-defense puzzle is proper technique. Of all the components that make up a properly executed defense sequence, this is the most important. You can have amazing speed, an excellent sense of timing, or even incredible power and strength, but if a technique is off, good luck making it work. Proper technique is your ultimate goal. It will prevail even without a lot of power, strength or speed. When you have attained proper technique, your martial sequence will work almost effortlessly.

Strength can be an amazing asset but not the most important one. In fact, strength can have its weakness, as ironic as it may sound. I used to train with a guy who was a power lifter. Let's call him Aaron. He was incredibly strong and had an inflated sense of his martial prowess because of his unnatural strength. When it came time to spar, he would typically dominate because he depended upon his strength and overpowered his weaker opponents. But anytime this man had to spar with someone who also had incredible strength, he always lost. I once watched him spar with a person much smaller and far weaker. Aaron was dominated. He received a pants-down spanking from his opponent because this guy had proper technique. Aaron's strength was no match for a smaller opponent with better technique. The smaller opponent frustrated Aaron so much that his strength waned quickly. He was toyed with like a piece of putty.

If you are incredibly strong, that is fantastic. Be proud of that asset. But remember that there's always someone out there stronger than you. What happens if the fight drags on and you get tired? Your strength will leave you. If that strength is all you are depending on, you will be disappointed. Proper technique will prevail. If you took two opponents that are equal on all fronts but one had better technique, obviously, the opponent with better technique will prevail. Proper technique is of paramount importance.

I remember my first exposure to a sensei who really knew proper technique. Other students were applying this particular arm lock to me and it wasn't hurting very much. This was causing me to lose respect for the move and, therefore, respect for the technique. When the sensei came around and applied this seemingly same arm lock on me, it was immensely painful. I was transported into a world of pain. It was tremendously effective. And all he did was apply the technique with a few modifications (some slightly different angles) and the difference was like night and day. It became self-evident that the subtle differences do, in fact, make all the difference in the world. They are what make proper technique, and proper technique is what all serious martial artists strive for.

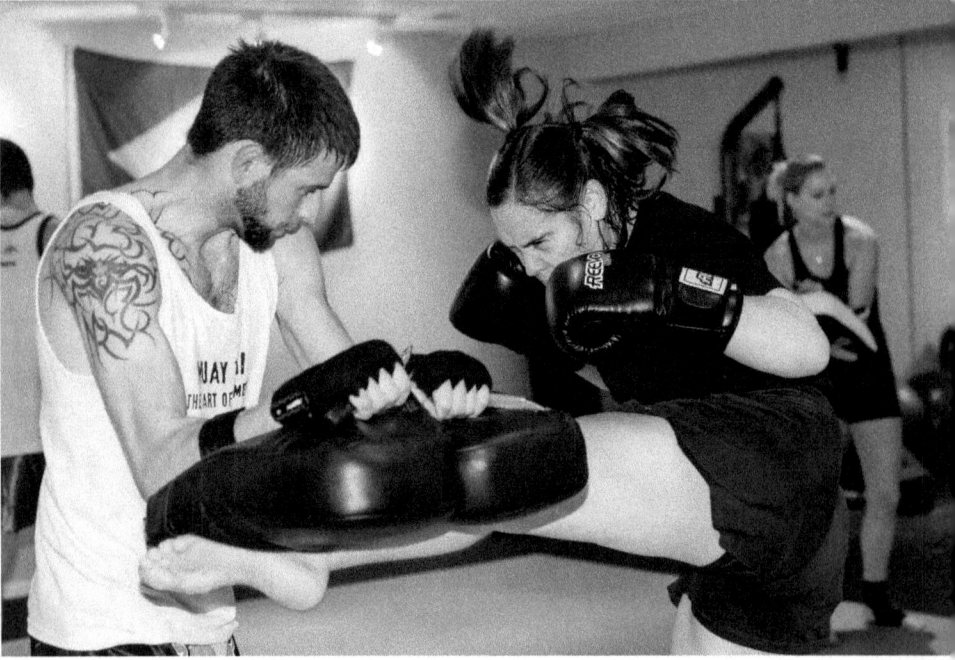

Chapter 13

The Best Way to Attain Amazing Technique

Change up your approach. Change up your training sessions. Do not always practice your self-defense sequence in the same manner. Consider even not training at full speed or full force all the time. Break the martial sequence down into its component parts and train them individually. Think of it this way. If the very first move of the self-defense sequence that you want to train is a lead leg push kick/foot jab/teep, training just the first part of the sequence, the kick, will improve that one aspect. It's like taking the individual technique out and shining it up and putting a high polish onto it so that when it's placed back into the sequence, the entire arrangement is improved or elevated.

In one training session, train just the entry of the sequence. You know the stimulus that is applied or directed at you that causes you to launch or start your defensive action. Train different stimulus that trigger the event. Train different angles; change it up so that your technique becomes more versatile and applicable in slightly different situations. Train it against different equipment to hone particular attributes.

Let's take that front kick we were talking about earlier. Train it in the following varying ways:

- Have a partner hold the heavy bag so that you can kick into it with full force. You are developing the power aspect of the kick. Remember that you are kicking "through" your target, aiming at a point deep inside the heavy bag and not merely the surface.
- Now train your focus and accuracy. Have your partner hold a focus mitt on the area you're targeting on his body. Perform the same kick, although, this time, do not worry about developing power. Kick the target much lighter than before, but with 100% accuracy. This time, you are developing your accuracy and focus.
- So what about timing? Have your partner put on a heavy chest protector. Now have him stand in the outside range and move towards you with the attack. Slowly, at first, time your kick so that you meet his incoming momentum with the outgoing force of your kick. You practice this over and over again so that your kick contacts with just the right timing. Correct timing means it doesn't knock you backwards at all. You deliver 100% of the love into your opponent.
- Now take off all that gear and place that kick with 100% accuracy against your opponent, but this time, practice control. Do not hit him hard at all but do make contact.

Take each individual component of your sequence and train it in this manner. You will put a high gloss on the entire sequence and your technique will develop a razor-sharp edge.

Getting your martial technique to top-notch level is not rocket science. It's just dedication, perseverance and training with the most efficient methods. Find yourself all of the above and you will be on your way to awesome technique in no time.

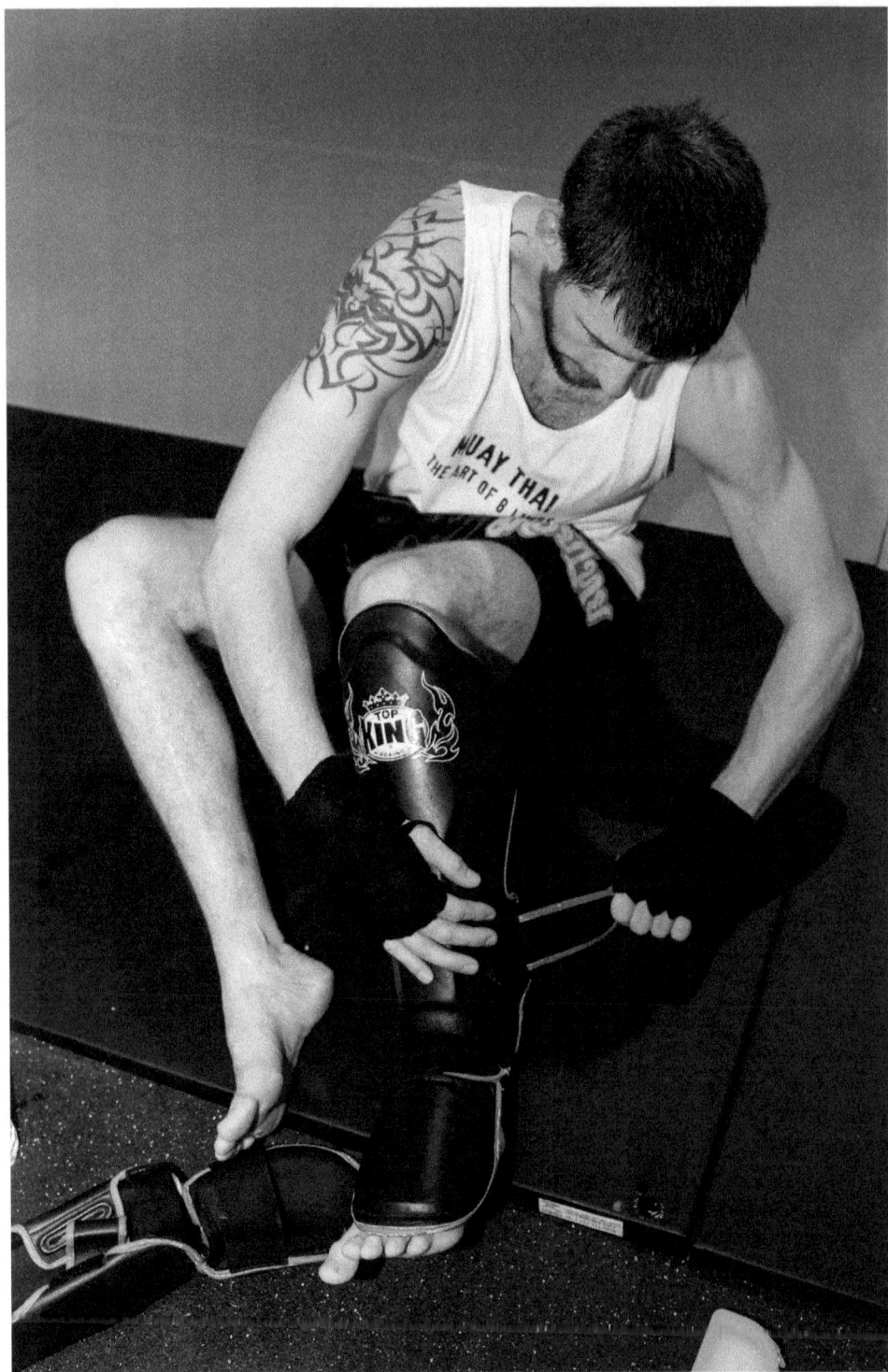

Chapter 14

Is Your Confidence Justified?

One of the worst offenses you can commit against yourself in the martial arts is becoming full of false confidence. How many times have you heard about the black belt that got his butt kicked by some untrained individual? I have personally met black belts who probably couldn't defend themselves very well at all. Or how about black belts teaching self-defense when they've never had to fend off an attacker? I think it's great if you have never had to fight but to teach self-defense without ever having to use the very tactics you are teaching is a little strange.

Consider the people who have only taken a self-defense seminar and then feel complete confidence in defending themselves. That might be a bit misguided. There's nothing wrong with an instructor holding a woman's self-defense class of one or two sessions. But walking away from one of these events if that is all the training that you've received can be more dangerous than not having attended the class in the first place. This all depends on the material covered in class, of course.

I have taught self-defense classes that were only a few sessions long but they contained mostly information on how to avoid confrontation. I also added a few tried-and-true physical techniques but the information dealt with situational awareness. This is the best information you can give someone if he is only going to dedicate a few hours to his entire self-defense plan. It's extremely difficult to learn a complicated self-defense sequence well enough in one class to use it against an aggressive attacker. This can give you a sense of false confidence, of false security. Please don't misunderstand me. It is great to offer these courses and I applaud the instructor who does. Just keep the complicated moves out of it.

Self-defense tools can fill a person with false confidence. Take pepper spray or a taser for instance. If you depend on these devices to save your life, I have a few questions for you. Do you have them with you everywhere? How about under your pillow or in your handbag? Do you have them at the beach while you're ready to enjoy a swim? Will they even work for you? Are the batteries of your taser always charged? If you have been carrying your pepper spray for two years, how do you know the pressure hasn't slowly leaked out over time? And all this while, it was just the pepper leaking out that made your nose run and not real cold symptoms.

I'm not even going to entertain the absolutely valid argument that these self-defense tools can be taken away from and used against you. As you can see clearly, there are far too many questions to answer here. Having these tools would be a great compliment against multiple attackers or a larger drug-crazed assailant if you are trained in their proper use, but depending on them is a very dangerous game.

Confidence is a great thing to have. Simply displaying the attribute can help you avoid being on the victim selection list that mugger has in his head. But, for your sake, I hope that confidence is backed by training.

Photo Contributed by Author

Chapter 15
When Your Back Is Against the Wall

The instructor yelled, "Fight!" Standing in front of me was a much more experienced student. Through the visor of his motorcycle helmet I could see the intensity in his eyes. He was wearing fully-padded sleeves, chest protection and 14 oz red Everlast boxing gloves. The instant the instructor yelled fight, those gloves started swinging at my head in a flurry. Red fists of fury. This was the first time I had sparred absolutely full contact. We were both wearing motorcycle helmets and some pretty cool padding so we could beat on each other pretty hard without fear of serious injury. It was the first of many such sparring sessions.

The above scenario may sound extreme to some of you who practice the martial arts. But unless you have been in several real-life situations that required self-defense, you absolutely must train at least some of the time at full intensity. How can you expect to react in a self-defense situation with deadly serious intensity if you don't train with those same emotions in the dojo from time to time?

Not training with enough intensity, or hell, never having had to use your techniques in a real situation, can be a serious threat to your safety. If you've never used it, how do you know for sure that it will work for you? I am not suggesting you intentionally seek out a violent confrontation to test your skill. That would be ridiculous. But you must engage in serious stress inoculation while training. You must know how you would act when facing a confrontation. Added pressure like a crowd watching or mass attack training to get your heart rate up or training full-intensity like what I described above is a close way to find out. This is the type of training you want to perform on a regular basis. Yes, you must occasionally train with incredible intensity. Just be sure not to overdo it so you don't burn out.

There is another way to experience the stress of a physical altercation. Get paid to do it. The following advice will not be acceptable to many but I offer it as it has served me tremendously well.

I had not been in a physical altercation in over five years so the idea of working as a bouncer at a local bar was intriguing. The head bouncer was a black belt at the Ju-Jitsu club I trained at so getting the job was easy. He asked, I accepted. The second night I was working, I ejected my first patron. I was nervous at the idea of employing some kind of lock or hold on a violent drunk as I had never done it before. When the moment arrived, it seemed almost as if in slow motion. He was yelling at some guy. I walked up beside him, grabbed his arm and simply bent his wrist into the lock. By the time he noticed what was happening, turning his attention towards me, it was too late. The lock was tightened, he was on his tippy-toes and he walked in a very compliant manner to the front door.

Wow, my first physical altercation in many years! The year that followed had many stories of successful conflict resolution scenarios at that bar. Every bouncer came from the same Ju-Jitsu club and we trained together. We were a tight team of martial arts practitioner bouncers who knew we could depend on one another.

Whether you are in the thick of it during the course of your vocation or simulating high-stress self-defense scenarios at your training hall, you react the way you train. So train hard and with appropriate intensity.

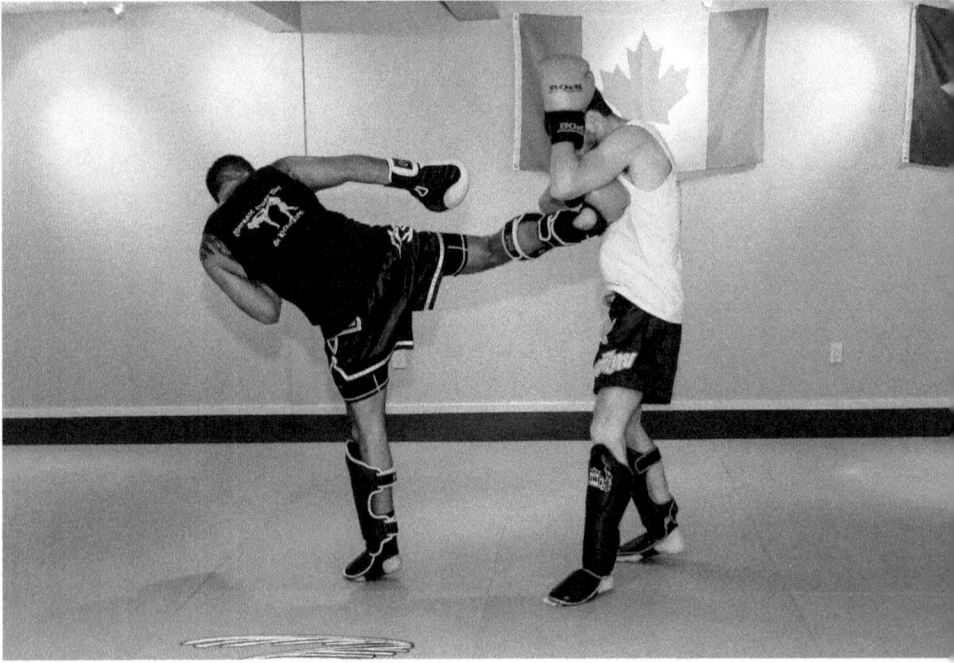

Chapter 16
Persistent Pain

As trained martial artists, we know that each individual technique in our self-defense sequence has a purpose. Nothing is an insignificant warm-up act before the big show. Each part of our defensive sequence has a definite purpose and they all share a similar quality. That quality is pain.

It hurts to engage us at every point of contact.

Paul Vunak had a great way of explaining this. Once, we stayed at Tom Cruise's house in Santa Margarita, California and trained in his garage. For five days in a row, all day long, we trained with Paul and Tom. One of the main concepts that we were taught over and over was the idea that every time your opponent tries something on you, it hurts them. He said, "Every time you put a body part out towards me, it's like getting an electric shock or being stung by a bee. You go to kick me, it will hurt you." He then raises his knee or shin to demonstrate how he would intercept your kick. "You go to punch me and you get stung." He then demonstrates an elbow destruction or a gunting.

Paul continued to explain the concept that your opponent can experience a degrading effect on their morale when **everything hurts** while attempting to make physical contact with you.

Another huge benefit of arming yourself with techniques that by themselves can cause real pain or serious damage is the idea that every technique in your self-defense sequence on its own can be enough to end the confrontation. Have you ever watched a boxing match or perhaps a fight on YouTube that was over with just one good stiff jab? I have. That's one blow and you're done.

When we break our self-defense sequence down and train each individual technique to get the maximum love out of it, that's when we're training properly. Take that stiff jab, for instance. When was the last time you focused on just training your jab? First, train the jab with shadow boxing using visualization. Then train to develop power by over-exaggerating your body movement and pushing it deep into the heavy bag. Next, train speed with your partner holding focus mitts. Then train targeting by having him move around while you smack that mitt dead center. Then it's back to the heavy bag again to put it all together. Did you work both sides equally? When's the last time you really focused on training just one of the basics?

Before you think that you don't need to train your basics because you have been in the arts for a while now, remember the following words.

"I fear not the man who has practiced 10,000 kicks once, but I fear the man who has practiced one kick 10,000 times." – Bruce Lee

There you have it. Train with the mindset that every bit of contact with you in a confrontation will hurt your opponent. Each technique of yours must be carefully honed to bring out the best of it against someone who would do you harm. And when someone does make the mistake of forcing you into a physical confrontation, make it hurt.

Chapter 17
A Purpose of Pain

To the novice martial artist or an untrained individual, he would probably think of pain in terms of a throbbing, sharp or dull pain or even a general or nagging pain. These would be the words he would use to describe it. Most people certainly think of it as something that they do not want to experience. To the trained martial artist, however, we understand that pain is one of the greatest motivators we have at our disposal to achieve our objectives during a potentially violent confrontation.

Human beings instinctively move away from pain and towards pleasure. The stronger motivating force is pain of course, and getting away from it becomes our top priority when experiencing it. Understanding this concept, we can use this knowledge to our advantage.

"How so?" you may ask. To the skilled martial artist, pain has direction. We realize it has tremendous value once understood properly. Previously, you read about how every point of contact with us hurts the attacker. This understanding of pain allows us to achieve this in many efficient ways.

Take an inner bent wrist lock for example. When slowly applying this lock to an individual, you can see the structural chain of events taking place. First, you see the elbow move. Then the shoulder dips. Then both shoulders move as the body trunk moves away from the pain. Once fully locked, only a very slight movement on your part will cause your opponent to move just where and how you want them to. Move the wrist in one direction and the opponent adjusts his body in an attempt to lessen the pain he experiences.

I was involved in a Ju-Jitsu demonstration many years ago on the topic of how to get the choke even when your opponent is protecting his neck. I was mounted and, as per the demo, I turned on my stomach and did my best to protect my neck. The guy on top of me dug his thumb in behind my jaw into my mandibular nerve just behind my ear. It hurt so much that, in spite of the pressure with my face pressed firmly on the mat, I turned my head while gouging a section of skin out of my forehead! You see, I had my left hand on the mat, my face on my left hand, and my right hand was protecting my neck. As he turned my head, my forehead scraped across my wedding ring and gouged out a section of skin.

At this exact moment, all I cared about was moving my head away from the excruciating pain of the mandibular nerve pressure. As my head turned, the choke was applied. The point of using directional pain to achieve your objective was sharply made.

Of course, this is just one example to show that understanding how the directional element of pain can benefit the trained martial artist. Learn this well and your ability to end conflict fast and efficiently will be greatly improved.

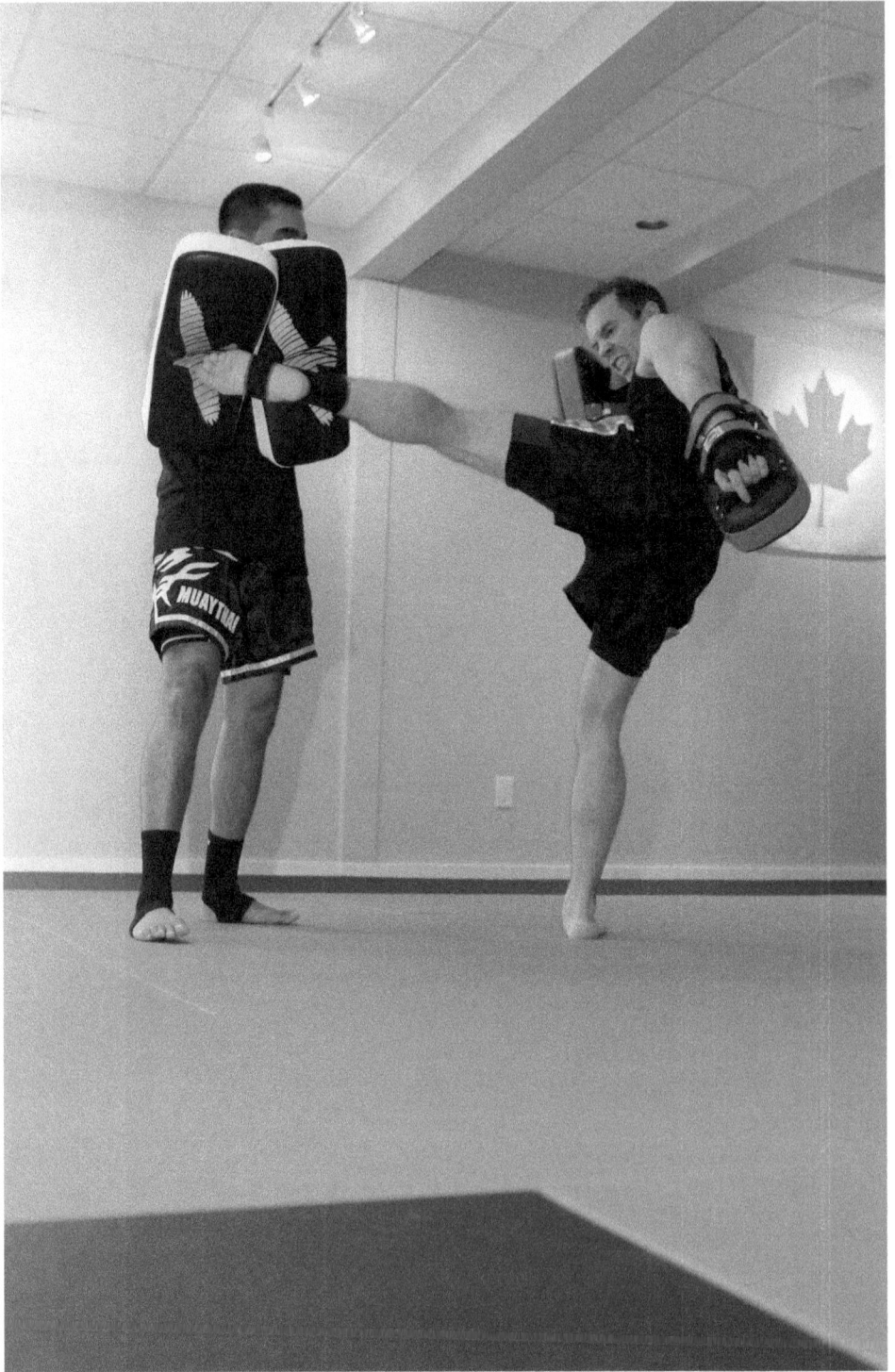

Chapter 18
How to Achieve Mystical Martial Power

I remember when it happened for the first time. I was at work and was leaving the factory floor to enjoy a well-deserved break when I was suddenly "attacked" from behind. Someone snuck up behind me and was rapidly closing the distance in an attempt to "pants" me. That's right, they were going to yank my pants down as some form of silly practical joke. Without even thinking, I parried the reaching hand and was just in the process of simultaneously inner bent wrist-locking the offending right hand while starting to lunge towards her face with the top of my head. I was about to launch a brutal head-butt to complement the wrist lock.

Several things occurred to me at once. The first and most startling thing was the fact that this course of action never entered my conscious thought process. I was merely observing it unfold before me without even thinking about it. The second immediate thought was that the head-butt would have been entirely inappropriate with this practical jokester. Before you wonder much longer, no, I did not complete the head-butt. She did whine a bit about her wrist, but for the next week or more, she kept warning people, "You don't want to sneak up on that guy."

My ego enjoyed the brief attention but the fact remained that I acted instinctively. I had trained many years to achieve the almost mystical level of acting without the mind. I trained in faith that the day would come, and here it was. It had arrived. I had achieved the "mind of no mind," Mushin no shin or, simply, Mushin.

I call it mystical because I did not understand how that happened. Now I do. I'd like to introduce you to your new friend Myelin, which was first introduced to me by productivity expert and my partner at WritersRise.com, Nick Brodd.

In his book, Nick writes about myelin and how it helps create habits and reinforce them. Myelin is a special layer of lipids and proteins that surround the nerves in the brain and the spinal cord. As the myelin sheath thickens, it becomes better at insulating and protecting your nerves. More importantly, it becomes more efficient at bolstering any habits you might already have. To thicken the myelin sheath around your nerves, you simply have to repeat an activity over and over again. The more you do it and get used to it, the more myelin becomes effective in reinforcing your habits until they become second nature, almost mystical to you.

When you hear a martial artist refer to muscle memory, he is actually referring to something that can now be measured with today's technological advances.

Consistency with your martial techniques will build your very own thought-less response. You will act instinctively and attain Mushin.

Photo Contributed by Author

Chapter 19
Blind Kung Fu Master?

You have probably seen at least one martial arts movie where a "blind" master was capable of incredibly amazing martial feats that would exceed even the most capable individuals with all of their senses intact. But this is just in the movies, right? It has to be all theatrics, correct? Guess again. Blindfolded or sight-deprived training can have tremendous benefits to the martial arts student.

Back in my Jeet Kune Do days, in the advanced class, we would sometimes grapple blindfolded. As strange as it may sound, we would even grapple in complete darkness. In a short period of time, you develop a more complete understanding of not just your opponent's physiology but your own as well. You quickly experiment with different angles while attempting to submit your opponent moving that wrist or elbow just slightly to get the lock to work better.

Years later, during my first black belt test in traditional Ju-Jitsu, my training partner Don and I practiced a blindfolded wrist lock series to demonstrate to the grading panel. You couldn't see a thing but once that hand grabbed your collar, it was on! The following locks were performed in sequence, all while blindfolded:

- Inner wristlock
- Thumb lock
- Outside twist bent wristlock/guided shark fin
- Straight arm lock
- Outer wristlock
- Inner wristlock come-along
- Clothesline
- Upper wristlock
- Upper spiral wristlock to inner bent takedown

Along with your chosen finishing technique, the above techniques represent no less than ten techniques in sequence where you manipulate your opponent without the benefit of your sense of sight. To make this all work, you have to sense your opponent's exact location and movement only by holding a small fraction of his body. This only becomes possible after a significant amount of experience and training with these moves. Experience tells you that once you apply force in one particular direction on your opponent's wrist, he will move in a certain direction. You can literally feel the tension increase or decrease in your partner's joints as you both move.

When deprived of sight, your sense of touch is heightened. You can literally feel that your opponent doesn't like what you are attempting. You can feel him jerk or move rapidly away from the pain. This gives you an instinctive sense of how to apply the locks or joint manipulations at a much deeper level, increasing your understanding and the improvement of your technique.

I am not suggesting you train in the dark daily. Vision-deprived training should be an activity that you participate in on a semi-regular basis. Give just a few months of once-a-week effort and you'll see just how rapidly your technique improves.

Chapter 20
Martial Mysteries Explained

I was your typical non-believer when it came to pressure points and control tactics. Just like my belief in ghosts, I needed to see it in order to believe it. Like most martial artists, I watched a lot of kung fu or martial arts movies. I would see these people perform amazing feats of martial arts theatrics. But surely these mystical martial powers are reserved only for the big screen, correct?

I had the privilege of training for a few years in the traditional martial arts as a teenager. Kempo karate was great for a young teen, teaching discipline and a solid sense of the basic martial arts techniques, not to mention instilling the training discipline at an early age. (Thank you, Beverly Dick.) One thing I failed to learn, however, was some of the amazing things I saw in movies, like the ability to stun people with seemingly light contact.

It's interesting to note that I had trained martial arts for over ten years before I knew anything specific about pressure points and nerve centers. Like my feelings towards Dim Mak or the death touch, I felt the idea of manipulating an opponent's nervous system to achieve shocking results was all bullshit. Jeez, I even had a book on the esoteric aspects of the ninja death touch where the author shows a detailed chart that tells exactly what time of day to strike a man in the chest to cause a certain type of effect. I found information like this to be rather amusing. Nothing at all to take seriously.

I am not putting Ninjutsu down in any way. Two years ago, I trained with a Ninjutsu instructor in Montreal. This guy was extremely skilled and one of the toughest guys I've ever met. (Thank you, Louie C.)

I still remember the day clearly. My JKD training partner Don and I walked into the Ju-Jitsu club for the first time. We met the chief instructor and quickly signed up for an introductory package. He was talking a little bit about manipulating nerve centers. I hoped he didn't notice my eyes starting to roll slightly as I thought, "Oh crap, here we go again. Another martial arts 'master' willing to take my money in exchange for teaching things that simply would not work on the street." Perhaps sensing my cockiness, the instructor invited me onto the mat and requested that I swing at him with a hook punch as fast as I wanted.

Did I punch him in the head?

He was standing, facing me in a ready stance; open hands, palms facing towards me. He blocked my hook punch with his hand extending just slightly past my head, and then he pulled his hand back towards himself and hit me behind my head squarely on the occipital, right at the back of the head on the base of the skull. That was the last moment I had control over my body. I saw an immediate flash and then felt as if I was being guided gently to the mat. I wasn't truly unconscious but I had no control over my arms or legs. By the time my control came back, my bicep was folded over my face, held firmly by his left hand. One of his knees had pinned my hips to the mat and I was 100% defenseless!

Here I was, an apprentice instructor in Jeet Kune Do, in addition to over seven years of traditional karate, and I was rendered completely helpless with one blow. And I wasn't even hit all that hard.

I was even more impressed when the chief instructor explained exactly what I had experienced in terms of human physiology. He used the term gross motor dysfunction to describe what caused me to slip from my consciousness just enough to render me defenseless. It was law enforcement veteran

Bruce Siddle who developed the Nerve Pressure Point Control Tactics System. Using this system, you can cause a gross motor dysfunction by striking nerve points along the body. This impact causes the muscles to temporarily weaken, just enough to impair your opponent. I was now a believer.

Chapter 21
The Right Martial Stuff

You can find martial arts clubs where two individuals can be training partners and move through the entire curriculum from white belt to black belt without ever having to train with anyone else. Now this may be great for you to get your black belt in an expeditious way, but it is not doing you any favors at all. You need to be able to practice your technique against all sorts of different opponents—fat ones, tall ones, short ones, long arms, short arms, stocky with low center of gravity, tall with high center of gravity, etc. You need to train against different skill levels and styles as well. It is only after training with a wide variety of individuals that you gain the understanding and experience needed to defend yourself in a wide variety of scenarios.

You understand the appeal, of course. A semi-timid individual wants to get his black belt. He has had the goal ever since he was a child and saw a movie where a smaller man defeated many foes with almost mystical power. The bullies had no chance and, at the end of the movie, the guy got the girl. It's a wonderful image. So now our adult chooses a martial arts club that will allow him to get his black belt without too much interaction from others. In fact, he is permitted to train with one partner and only that partner. Both learn each other's subtleties, balance, skill level, and mannerisms and, in no time, are moving across the mat with grace and flow. They cooperate with each other and all their techniques work flawlessly.

A false sense of ability.

The day finally arrives. They invite family and friends to witness their black belt exams. It goes off okay and they achieve black-belt status. A life goal achieved. Sounds absolutely terrific, doesn't it? They are black belts now, capable of almost mystical martial abilities, right? Guess again. I have seen black belts go to a different school and get schooled by much lower-ranking belts. This is a shame.

How do you avoid this martial mistake? A great martial experience of mine was training at the Creative Fighter's Guild in Penticton, British Columbia. Almost every class, we would be drilling and the instructor would yell, "Change!" or bang two sticks together very loudly. Upon this signal, we would immediately change partners. You would grab whoever was closest to you and continue the drill. In a relatively short period of time, you could pull off your techniques or make your techniques work against everybody. When it came time to spar, it didn't matter if the guy in front of you was big and strong, or small, wiry and fast. You had experience in training with this body type. There is great value in this training method.

I have had the privilege of training at both types of clubs. I have witnessed the incompetent black belt factory. I have also witnessed clubs like the one described above and several clubs in between.

Know thyself. What is the ultimate reason you decided to train in the first place? The answer to that question dictates the kind of club you train at.

Chapter 22

Hitotsu-Tachi: One Stroke, One Cut

Swordsmen from Japan have often endorsed the idea of "one cut" or "one stroke." They believe that through very serious devotion to the art of swordsmanship they can develop attributes such as speed, timing, accuracy and complete commitment that they could end the confrontation with only one cut if executed properly. That is one blow to end the fight.

Few swordsmen in history embodied this ideal more than Tsukahara Bokuden. This man fought in over 30 battles and engaged in 20 to 30 duels, depending on the books you read. What truly describes the concept of "one cut" is the idea that you wait until the last possible moment of your opponent's attack and, with blinding speed, you launch your counterattack and literally beat your opponent to the punch. What complicates things is the notion that your opponent's sword would miss you by less than an inch. Your full commitment and energy is on your attack, not in avoiding the enemy's attack. Now this is 100% commitment to your self-defense.

How can we use this concept and absorb what is useful? A quick search online can reveal fight videos where the fight seemed to be over almost before it began, like what we previously discussed about fights ending with just a stiff jab. It is completely possible to achieve this. With the mindset of moving towards embodying the modern samurai, train each technique as if that one technique alone would be enough to end the fight.

Our self-defense sequences typically contain many moves strung together in a clever manner designed with the sole intention of making it impossible to overcome once we seize the initiative. Train these moves with the mindset the samurai had hundreds of years ago. Train with the idea of hitotsu-tachi—one cut, one stroke. Train with the understanding that even if you are feigning your opponent, you don't merely flinch the move in some half-assed attempt to distract. You show a complete start to the move, the drive. It is very real until it is pulled away at the last possible moment and your next technique scores a full-power hit.

Training with 100% commitment to each and every technique will develop within you the ability to end the confrontation with one stroke, one cut, one blow.

Yes, our defensive sequence almost always contains several techniques. When you train with the above mindset, when you give 100% commitment to your self-defense, you will find that you never get to the end of the sequence. Your attacker has crumbled before you reach your last move. This, of course, is our ultimate goal.

Clear your mind. Train with 100% commitment. Make each action count and be 100% committed to your chosen tactics once unleashed.

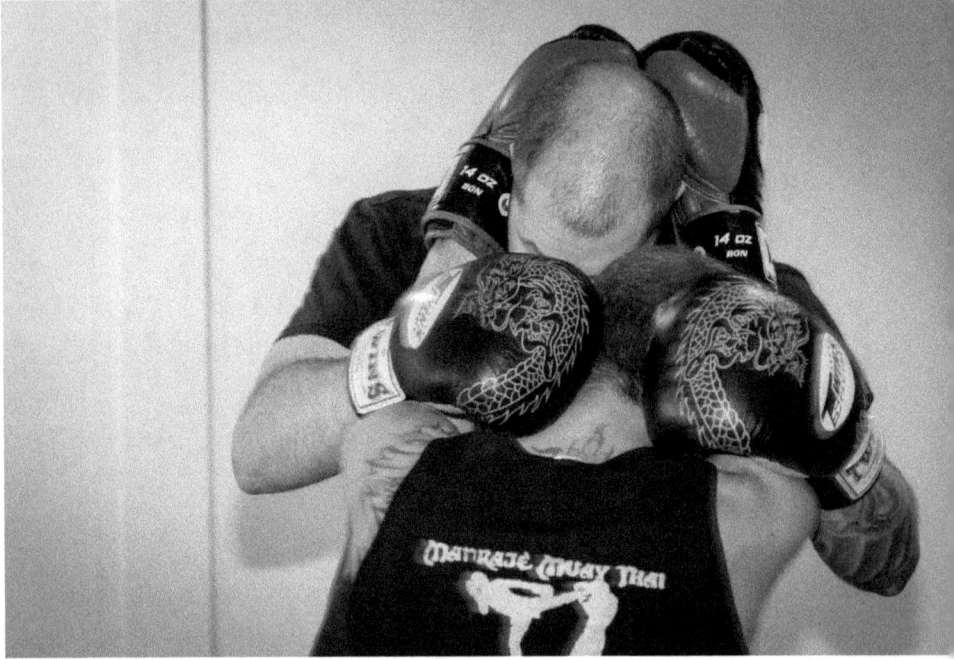

Chapter 23
The Violent Truth

Every once in a while, either in class or during a discussion regarding self-defense, a student or the person I was speaking with will get the wrong idea about the genuine existence of violence in the world today. When discussing appropriate response to a violent attack, they make comments along the lines of "Well, I just couldn't harm another human being in that way," or "I'm just not the kind of person who enjoys hurting others". As if the reason you are training in the martial arts is practicing to harm others. As if your main motivation is to cause another person pain.

This is a misguided perspective.

Quite the opposite is true. As modern samurai, we pursue the path of non-violence. We always strive to avoid a violent encounter for a variety of reasons. Our end game is ultimately becoming good citizens, good people who are contributing members of society, people who have a skill-set to help others in their time of need.

Some of us tend to see others through our own eyes, the eyes of "generally good people". The problem arises in the assumption that everyone is good, believing that everyone you encounter on the street is just like you. Every single one of them would never dream of hurting an innocent or imposing their will on another human. Sadly, this is simply not the truth.

Whether it is because of an addiction to a serious substance, a genuine mental imbalance or just a plain propensity for evil acts, some people have little internal resistance to the idea of torturing small animals, hurting humans or other unpleasant realities. There are psychopaths out there.

If I offered you a $100 bill and 60 seconds on a search engine right now, you can find countless examples of terrible things that happened to good people at the hands of individuals who "seemed so quiet."

I do not offer this position to make you jaded towards strangers or curtail your interaction with people you don't know. I write this as a reminder to train with the correct mindset.

Try this. Next time you hit the heavy bag, pause for a moment, close your eyes and envision what your attacker has in store for you at the conclusion of his attack. Is it humiliation? Domination? Is it worse? Visualize the situation and train with full purpose.

You must launch your self-defense sequence with full commitment to stop the attack and prevent further attack. Your attacker doesn't care about you in the least. Your primary concern should be on getting home safe. Anything less than full commitment to stopping this person with whatever means at your disposal possible is simply not acceptable.

After all, the moment your attacker cannot attack you any longer, you will stop. This is probably more consideration then they will show you. You are in the right. Have you worked out your self-defense strategy ahead of time?

Chapter 24

The Throttle-Back Factor

The samurai subscribed to the philosophy of mutual destruction. They did not fear the possibility of death when going into battle. Imagine how much easier it would be to defeat your opponent if you didn't care at all whether you got hurt or not. The students of today, without this mindset, place restrictions on their techniques and tactics. I'm not suggesting that we, the modern samurai, need to adopt the philosophy of mutual destruction. But we do need to solve with our newer students a problem I call the throttle-back factor.

To the beginner, it makes complete sense not to hit something as hard as you can with your closed fist. You are a beginner, after all, and you may not know how to hit without causing yourself at least a little damage. The human body instinctively protects itself from damage. Thousands of years ago, if you damaged yourself even slightly, life could become extremely difficult. It could even result in your death. It is just part of our survival instinct to not want to hurt ourselves.

When you subconsciously pull back your strike before it even hits your opponent, when you throttle back , you fail to deliver full force. This is not 100 percent commitment to your self-defense. This can cause your opponent to lose respect for your ability and come at you even harder.

But when a new student wraps his head around the prospect of taking all those tiny bones in his fingers, in his hand, and in his wrist and form all of that into a fist to make a striking implement, and then contemplate striking one solid bone, like his opponent's skull, it just doesn't make sense. It's like punching a rock, not something they want to start off doing full force.

Of course, one of the ways we solve this issue is to teach the new student to use the correct tool for the job. Fists strike soft targets. Elbows, knees, the heel of your palm can strike the harder surfaces, like the head.

Some martial arts solve this problem by literally transforming the human body into a weapon. They employ repeated striking or striking various substances and surfaces to increase bone density and transform your fists into clubs. .All this striking brings the student's confidence level up and decreases the urge to throttle back. However, it should be mentioned that the kind of individual who would endure this style of training for the amount of years necessary to turn his body into a weapon would not be the kind of individual that would throttle back in the first place.

Learn from the samurai of the past. Learn the attitudes that they embraced and apply it to our times today. This is what being the modern samurai is all about.

Chapter 25
Your Unwavering Code

When reading about the samurai code, you will often find references and quotes that demonstrate the samurai's loyalty to his family. You also learn that, as modern samurai, transforming yourself into a good citizen and a contributing member of society, you cannot attain this without first establishing an unshakable sense of virtue. A value system, in other words.

A moral code makes decision-making very easy. When faced with a moral dilemma, you simply ask yourself, "Is what I am contemplating at the moment aligned with or against my moral code?" The answers become self-evident. Having a well-established value system is your foundation and it starts at home. It starts with respect for your family and basic house rules.

Consider the following quote from Takeda Shingen, a nobleman in Japan circa 1521-1573 AD. While discussing the samurai, he said, "One who was born in the house of a warrior, regardless of his rank or class, first acquaints himself with a man of military feats and achievements in loyalty... Everyone knows that if a man doesn't hold filial piety toward his own parents, he would also neglect his duties toward his lord. Such a neglect means a disloyalty toward humanity. Therefore such a man doesn't deserve to be called 'samurai.'"

A foundation must be solid and true. It doesn't matter whether we are talking about self-defense techniques or your moral code. The foundational material must be reinforced with repetition and purpose. All of the greatest fighters, or athletes for that matter, attribute their success to mastery of the basics. A common mistake made by junior students of the martial arts is subscribing to the idea that they must always be learning new techniques.

Have you ever been to a seminar where the instructor steps out onto the mat and begins to throw technique after technique at you? You struggle to try a few repetitions of the lock but then it's on to the next one. "Okay, you guys, here is the next move in the progression," the instructor yells. You do your best to remember the moves but they keep coming. At the end of the seminar, do you really remember any of the techniques? Probably not very many are retained.

Compare this to the training session where you work only on one move with perhaps a few variations. Not only can you make the move work at the end of the training session, you'll also do it tomorrow and the next day.

And so it is the same with one's moral code. Through constant reinforcement, making decisions in alignment with your moral code will become effortless and even without thought. A strong moral code is foundational for considering yourself a modern samurai. Learn from the past. Learn from those you respect and develop your own unwavering code. It will make many things so much easier. It will simplify things for you. Bruce Lee knew this when he said, "The art of Jeet Kune Do is simply to simplify."

Chapter 26

Grappling With Statistics

"90% of all street fights end up on the ground."

Certainly, you have heard this statistic before and undoubtedly it was from a ground fighting or grappling student, enthusiast or instructor. What they really mean is that the overwhelming majority of fights that they are in end up on the ground. They say this because that is exactly what they train to do: get the fight to the ground. And who could blame them, really? This is their area of expertise. This is where they have the best chance at success, the best chance of winning the fight.

Sure, you've probably witnessed two drunken, out-of-shape guys fighting. They don't really know what they're doing so they end up kind of hugging each other and occasionally trying to punch each other in the head. It is usually when one of the men tries to punch the other in the head that the other guy moves suddenly, causing them both to lose their balance and fall to the ground. They roll around a bit until one of them gets lucky and ends up in the mounted position. He then rains down a few punches to the head and the fight is over.

These men were not prepared.

Although I can't cite a real study that accurately tells you how many fights do in fact end up on the ground, I am sure it's significantly less than the nine out of ten that we're led to believe.

Unless, of course, you consider that when a guy gets knocked out, he falls to the ground. But let's face it, the ground is a range of combat.

For you to be able to proclaim self-defense proficiency, you must know how to do many things if and when the fight takes you off your feet. You must learn more than just avoiding the takedown, avoiding getting mounted or having your opponents hands "tied up." When was the last time you trained while on the ground, grappling to access and open the folding knife that you carry? (Thanks Ole F.!) When was the last time you trained a two-on-one scenario while on the ground?

To become well-rounded in self-defense, you must train all ranges of combat. If you don't like the idea of having to change your training routine to accommodate learning grappling, too bad. Take yourself out of your comfort zone. At the very least, learn some serious takedown defenses, ground movement basics and how to get back up on your feet as fast as possible.

For the sake of self-defense, the ground is the last place you want to be. How do you defend yourself against two people while you're on the ground? How do you maintain situational awareness when someone is pressing his chest on your head, obscuring your vision?

For self-defense, you don't want to be on the ground at all. And that is exactly why you must train there.

Chapter 27
Tip Your Cup

If you have the opportunity to attend a seminar where different styles will be represented, I encourage you to attend. It is dangerous to train only in one club all the time with the same students, same instruction, same environment and the same discussion.

I'm not suggesting that you abandon your current club or even to train at more than one club simultaneously. Some instructors consider this inappropriate. It's seen as a sign of disrespect. What I'm suggesting you do is keep an open mind. Consider the old cliché of the empty cup.

"The usefulness of the cup is its emptiness." - Bruce Lee

While qualifying for my current security license, there were several people on the mats demonstrating their proficiency of the control tactics we were learning. One rather large gentleman would continually offer up "better" ways to execute the techniques. He would constantly refer to his many years in this style and that style. "This way works better," he would say as he resisted learning anything new from the instructor. As a matter of fact, if you had just walked into the room, you may have thought this guy was one of the instructors, not a student. On and on he droned about how much better and more effective his moves were at achieving the objectives. He wasn't even practicing the techniques demonstrated. He wasn't giving them a chance.

We were meant to practice the techniques presented, but I observed this guy performing moves that were completely different from what the instructor was showing. He was simply using the moves he already knew rather than learning the material presented.

By the end of the day, he did pass the course but relied on his size and strength and a very tired opponent. But the fact remains that he didn't learn anything new that day. He wouldn't even try the moves presented because of his "vast experience". How could he have learned anything at all? Nothing else would fit into his cup because it was already full.

I will be the first to admit that not everything taught that day was top-notch or cutting-edge technique. But there was some good stuff there. There were even a few ideas I was able to take and blend into my personal arsenal of favorite techniques and tactics.

Always keep an open mind.

A mentor of mine calls this zero-based thinking. Do not prejudge. Try to see things from all angles. Seek out its usefulness, incorporate that into your practice and disregard what doesn't fit.

Chapter 28

I Can't Be Taken To the Ground

My mouth dropped open. Did I just hear him correctly? A black belt in traditional Ju-Jitsu was standing on the mat instructing my training partner and I on control tactics. My partner Scott and I were training them rather vigorously when the black belt instructor walked up to us to offer some advice. He was demonstrating to us a modification to the move that he felt would improve it. Scott pointed out a flaw in his suggested technique that would expose us to being tripped very easily by a first-year wrestling student if we did it exactly as he suggested. When confronted with this critique, he quipped back, "Well, I can't be taken to the ground."

The man had a black belt in traditional Ju-Jitsu, not Brazilian Ju-Jitsu. It's not like he trained in grappling specifically, but he had a black belt in Ju-Jitsu. The sad fact was that he really knew very little about the ground game. Yet he had the arrogance to proclaim his superior prowess of Ju-Jitsu. Arrogance during a self-defense situation is dangerous indeed.

Sun Tzu gives us this advice: "Pretend inferiority, and encourage his arrogance."

Why would this advice be offered by perhaps the oldest known military strategist regarded by many as a strategy genius? Because arrogance will cause your downfall in a military battle as surely as it can in a self-defense situation. You cannot afford this attitude.

I remember a line in the samurai movie The Legend of Eight Samurai. It was something like, "The moment you feel you are invincible is the moment just before you fall." Sure, it's just a movie, but the wisdom holds true. An attitude that has you believing that you don't even have to consider an option in a fight means that you are not keeping an open mind. Your cockiness will have a price. Perhaps this guy was very skilled, but fights are rarely orderly. They rarely follow any rules. What if you tripped on the uneven surface outside or stumbled over the garbage can that was knocked over? There are many reasons the fight can go to the ground other than by a throw, trip or takedown.

You must keep a mind open to the unexpected. When you feel your mind closing, make a point of expressing to yourself sub-vocally, "I am observing myself thinking (the closed-minded thought.)" Then consider all possibilities to the situation. Open your mind to things that you would perhaps not even consider. Acknowledge them and their possibilities.

Do not allow yourself this mindset of arrogance. Train with all possibilities in mind. And remain humble.

Photo Contributed by Author

Chapter 29
Common Sense Self-Defense

Henry Ford is credited with the invention of the assembly line and, by extension, specialized labor. Since that time, as society advanced, jobs and the functions we perform in society have become much more specialized. As a result, we had to adapt in order to keep up.

All things considered, long gone are the days of the jack-of-all-trades. My grandfather, for example, was able to perform a great many functions in his day-to-day life. He owned and operated a farm. If the tractor broke down, he could make the repairs himself. In fact, he even had the ability to fabricate simple parts if needed. If an animal was injured or sick, he knew the basics on how to mend and nurse it back to health.

In fact, most of our grandparents and great-grandparents were far more self-reliant than the average person today. But that's progress, right? We are far better off today because of this, correct? You may argue, "We are much more productive now due to our advances." On some levels, I suppose this is true, but what is the price we pay for all this productivity?

Certain things, certain skills should be learned by all individuals. It doesn't matter how busy our lives get, there are basic skills that must be developed. What are these skills?

- Basic first aid - Do you know the basics to help keep someone alive until the EMT's arrive? How about how to stop bleeding? When and how do you put a sling? Can you give CPR?
- Basic healthy meal preparation - It's not enough knowing what foods are really good for you. You should also know what foods to limit or eliminate altogether.
- Correct use of your fire extinguisher - You do have at least one on every level of your dwelling, right? Certainly, you have a fire plan predetermined with your family ahead of time and practiced yearly, especially if you have children.
- Self-defense - You really want the ability to protect yourself against violent aggression.
- Basic swimming skills - Ensure you don't drown if you fall in a lake.

I'm discussing the basics here. You don't have to take the longest first aid course or enroll in culinary arts school. You just need to ensure that you do not become victimized by circumstances. After all, this is self-defense, common sense self-defense.

An old sensei of mine had a philosophy that I committed to memory: "No one is looking out for us other than ourselves. You must take responsibility for what has, is and will happen to you. We have the ability to do whatever we choose to do."

Don't bother arguing that the police are there to protect you against violent offenders. Aren't the police called after an attack? The fire department will show up only after the fire is raging. It is up to you to learn the skills necessary to mitigate any potential harm towards you or your family. It's up to you. The responsibility lies directly on your shoulders. Accept this, move forward and smile.

Society may be changing at a rapid pace and specialization may be advantageous to your career path, but certain life skills must be learned in order to join the ranks of the modern samurai. Take stock of what skills need a bit of polish in order to strengthen your overall strategy.

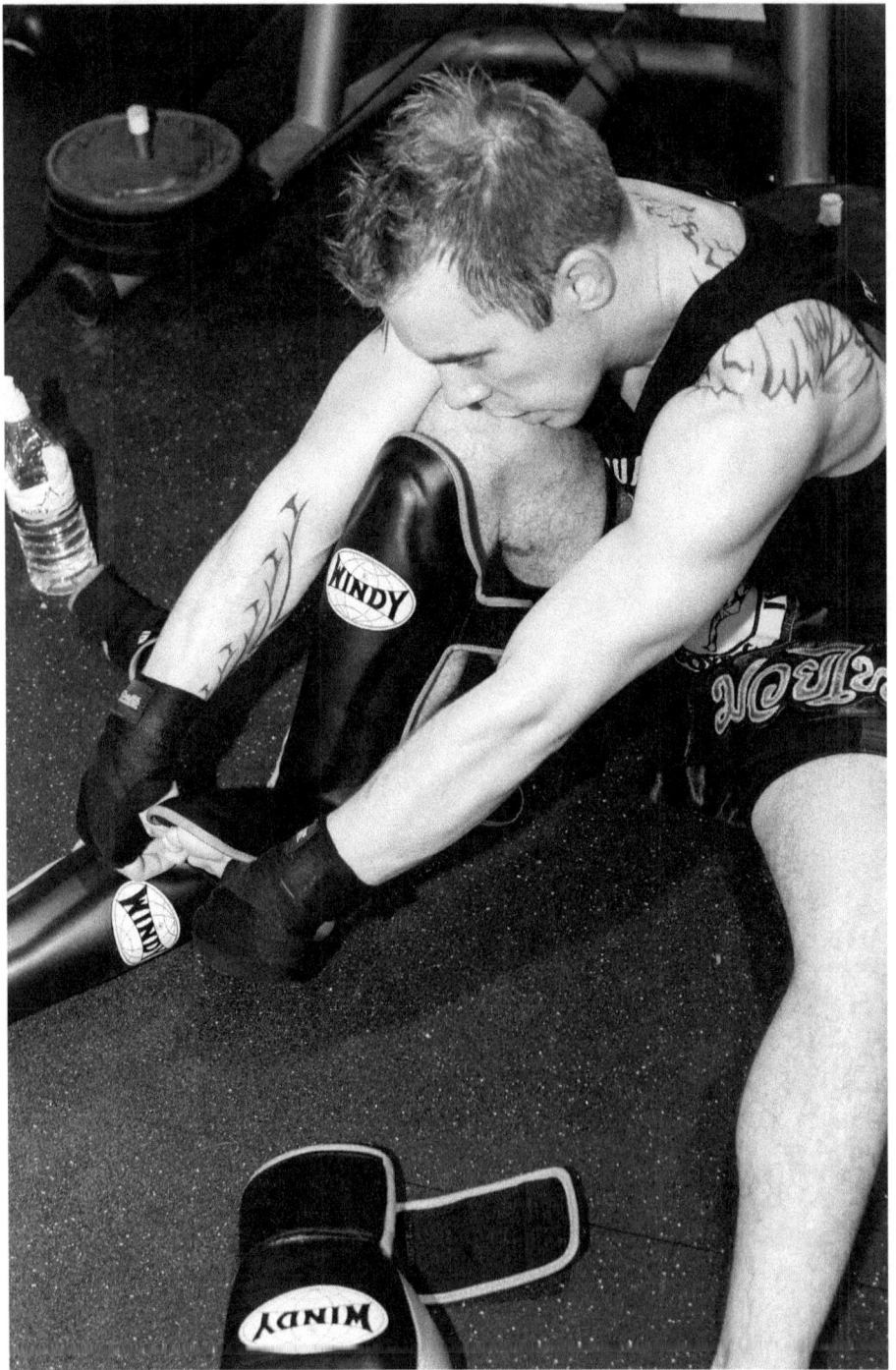

Chapter 30
Your Capable Calm

"So what would you do if somebody swings on you like this?"

I am sure you, as a martial artist, occasionally get asked questions like these. These questions are typically asked by people who have not spent much time, if any, in the martial arts. Because of their lack of experience in training the martial ways, they sometimes do not understand the answer that I provide. My answer is always, "I would respond instinctively. I would defend myself without having to think about it."

If the conversation progresses, and if the friend that I'm speaking with has a hard time believing or understanding how initiating one's self-defense sequence can occur as if on autopilot, I offer the following explanation.

Imagine you are driving home in your vehicle. You're in a residential neighborhood, and a child runs out from in between two parked cars. What do you do? You slam on the brakes, of course. You don't even have to think about this. It happens instinctively. Well, the same is true in the above scenario. Your arms are already moving up into defensive position as you begin to perceive the imminent physical threat. The thought process does not enter your conscious mind.

Let's break it down even further. An example of how this worked in my life was when I was working security one evening in a crowd. Without warning at all, some drunken jerk tried to sucker punch me. My response was a lead leg punch kick/teep to his lower abdomen, which opened up the double forearm shot to his brachials or the sides of his neck, then followed by a low knee. He crumbled to the floor unable to breathe for the next few moments. I even had more love to give him, but he had enough. That opening move, the kick, started my sequence.

Here's how one progresses through training to achieve your own calm, capable response to an attack. Here is the progression that allows you to act instinctively.

1. Unconscious incompetence
You have never trained before, so you are not even conscious of what to do in this situation. There are many moves available to the trained individual, but you don't even know that they exist.

2. Conscious incompetence
You have started training now. You have some moves at your disposal, but you are clumsy and awkward, and you have to concentrate on making them work against a training partner who is cooperating. At least, you now know what to do even if you can't make it work yet.

3. Conscious competence
You can make the move work now, but you require your full focus on what you are doing in order to make it work.

4. Unconscious competence
Now the technique flows from your body without conscious thought. You have achieved the ability to defend yourself without having to think about it. You simply defend yourself instinctively.

Of course, getting to the last level in the progression can take years of repetition and hard work, but it's worth the effort. Allow persistence to be your constant companion.

Chapter 31
The Pet Store Lesson

I needed pet food one day and decided to drive to the store to pick some up. The trip was thoroughly uneventful. While waiting in line to pay for the kibble, another man approached the register. "Holy cow, I haven't seen you in years!" was the first thing he said to me and I happily greeted an old friend.

We had a lot to catch up on, as it had been many years since we trained together at the same Ju-Jitsu club. Here we were, two individuals who both dedicated a good portion of our free time to the martial pursuits and who both possessed multiple black belts as a result, standing in line to pay for pet food. Our conversation continued outside of the store and while we stood on the sidewalk, this normal day turned into one with fantastic learning potential.

An overly loud conversation distracted our catching up as we turned to see three men walking through the parking lot. They were dressed as if they just got off some labor job. They wore stained clothing and carried lunch kits. One of the men had a hard hat. Two of them were obviously at odds with each other, yelling loudly now as they continued to walk directly toward us. The yelling progressed to shoving. A lunch kit hit the ground, and the first punch was thrown hitting the other man squarely on the side of his head.

Within a few very short moments many things happened. The men were now only 20 feet away, still moving towards the pet store's main entrance where we stood. My old friend and I stood there watching as the one punch turned to fists flying. A couple who had started to walk to the store, completely oblivious to what was happening, jumped back in fear at the sight of the two men fighting. A man walked out of the store and literally shrieked in horror and simply froze, unmoving. In fact, he was holding a cell phone and dropped it as he recoiled in fright. A young family in the parking lot ran away, and a store employee was looking out over the shoulder of the petrified man who was still frozen in the doorway. She commanded a fellow employee to "Call the police!"

What was interesting was that my friend and I both spent many years training and many years in the security industry. We both worked as bouncers together, breaking up fights exactly like this one. This was nothing new to us. This was nothing shocking. We stood there critiquing their terrible technique as the fight literally happened around us. Everyone else simply didn't know what to do. They didn't have a plan and they certainly weren't inoculated in any way to the potential stress of the violent situation unfolding right in front of them. At least the family man ushered his kids back to the car.

So which person would you be? Would you freeze in fear? Or would you have a plan?

Chapter 32
The Virtuous Path

Early on in a caterpillar's life the insect has within itself cells which lie dormant. These cells, at first, have no apparent meaning. They are called imaginal cells and contain all the instructions to create the butterfly that will emerge at some point in the crawling insect's life. What's interesting is that the caterpillar's own immune system actually attacks these cells at first, but the growth of the newer cells overcomes the old, and at last, a butterfly emerges.

This is a wonderful metaphor for those who seek all the martial teaching they can handle to train vigorously and with persistence, fulfilling an inner desire to grow as a martial artist and ultimately becoming that accomplished martial artist, the likes of which seemed almost unattainable at the beginning of their journey. As the caterpillar's immune system resisted the change at first, you too will encounter challenges along the martial path. But if the urge is strong enough, you will stay the course.

This kind of deep desire to learn as much as possible and progress in the martial arts is possessed by only a small percentage of students who first take up the pursuit.

Many people start training to lose a few pounds or gain some confidence. There are also those who have experienced some form of negative trauma or victimization at the hands of a bully, or worse. These individuals can be extremely motivated but there still is the distinction between them and those who just seem to have a deeper calling.

The best-case scenario is for a competent instructor or sensei to recognize this early on and nurture the spirit of the student to allow that persons own imaginal cells to reach his full expression; to achieve their martial ambitions. But just as the caterpillar's immune system could not prevent the butterfly's emergence, the student will progress with or without his instructor's help. This student will train wherever and whenever he can. She will train at home, hone her skills with friends and join multiple clubs simultaneously to gather the information she needs to fill her void.

These students can go on to become masters of their chosen art. These students even get drafted into better-established training clubs. And they go on to do very well in their field, whether it is in MMA fighting, becoming a renowned instructor or even becoming an ambassador of their style.

Each of us individually has our own imaginal cells urging us to progress and change. Are you listening to yours? What are they telling you? More specifically, which direction are they nudging you in? Do not be afraid to follow your passions. They will lead you to your destiny if you only listen and act accordingly. If listening to them has brought you to the martial path, welcome.

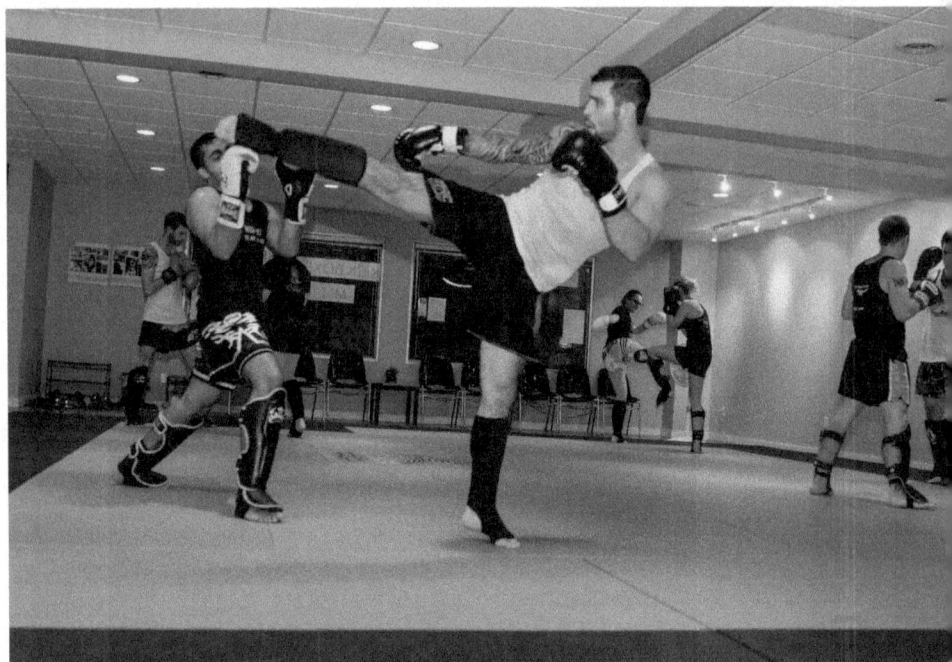

Chapter 33
A Lesson in the Art of Awareness

I was in Sacramento with a friend, whom we'll call Darren. We were both fairly young to be traveling from Canada, through the United States and into Mexico. But hey, what were two young adults to do when faced with a surprise two-week shutdown of our place of employment? Back to the story. We made several stops along the way and Sacramento just happened to be one of them. We were at some type of festival outside a bunch of shops. A crowd was enjoying the afternoon, and we were looking for a quick souvenir.

We noticed two guys talking and looking at us. Something wasn't right. Something was a bit out of the ordinary. They were paying too much attention to us. They split up and one walked directly at us. The one guy that split away from the other was still in view and it became clear that he was making his way in from behind us. The first man was right in front of us now talking loudly, asking us where we were from and becoming very animated with his hand gestures. The other guy came right up behind us and was trying to put his hand in our pockets!

What a crazy situation! It's not like we were in a third-world country with masses of kids trying to get something from us. This was the United States! We literally stood there facing each other so we could watch each other's backs, to warn of the close proximity of these scallywag pickpockets.

No, we weren't being physically assaulted but having your ID stolen in a foreign country can inconvenience your travel plans. Replacing an ID is more and more expensive, and there is also the potential cost of theft of identity. We got out of there as fast as we could, not wanting the situation to escalate, but a valuable lesson was learned.

What lesson, you ask? Thank goodness our martial arts instructors talked to us about situational awareness. We both trained in different styles of Karate at the time, but all self-defense styles teach situational awareness. The lesson of watching out for people who are watching you was thoroughly ingrained in each of us that, when we travel, we have a great many standard operating procedures we follow.

1. We carry secondary wallets. One wallet has a few dollars, some expired IDs, a few random business cards. That's it. I think Darren bought his for 0.50 cents at a garage sale. Somebody wants your wallet at gun or knife point? "Take it. That's all I have." Muggers don't want to stick around and count the money. They grab your stuff and run. Meanwhile, your real money and IDs are in your money belt.

2. We wrap a very thick rubber band around things we carry in our pockets. The rubber creates a friction you can feel when removing that item from your pocket.

3. We don't get overly intoxicated off the resort. This should not have to be mentioned but some tourists get in trouble every year getting drunk and found in places they shouldn't be in.

4. Avoid unfamiliar places at night.

5. Watch each other's backs and have a brief discussion with everyone on the safety practices to observe before the trip.

There are more, but this is a good start. Yes, most of the tips are common sense but most of us need a reminder from time to time. Safe travels.

Photo Contributed by Author

Chapter 34

Sixth-Sense
Self-Defense

It wasn't very warm that morning and the dew made the grass wet. I was avoiding the tall grass to keep my feet dry as I took my morning stroll into the forest. I was staying on a rural property only a short drive outside of the city. It was a beautiful property and part of its allure was the fact that the back property line bordered on Crown land. Crown land is land that the government owns here in Canada.

There are many established trails behind the property that were easily accessible just at the back property line. Locals ride their horses up there as there are miles upon miles of trails, making it excellent trail running territory. When heading out for a long run I would always carry some form of bear protection. That day, as it was just a very quick stroll, I took nothing.

I was approximately ten minutes into my walk and approaching a fork in the trail when, all of a sudden, the hair on the back of my neck literally stood on end. My entire scalp tingled. Even the hair on my arms stood at attention. Something clearly wasn't right. I stopped, looked around and listened. I sensed nothing, nothing with my five senses, that is. But still I knew something wasn't right. I listened to my instincts and crouched very low and remained quiet.

Then I heard it. The sound of branches breaking drew my attention up the trail and, at once, I was alerted to the reality of present circumstances. A sizable juvenile black bear was also on a morning stroll and walking toward me. My heart pounded and I scrambled to come up with a plan. Run? Fight? All I had with me was a modest fixed blade knife which wasn't even very sharp. I was much too far away from the sanctuary of the house or the protection of my rifle. I quickly assessed the wind direction and realized that the breeze was coming at both of us from the side. I concluded he couldn't smell me yet.

An overwhelming feeling directed me to stay put. Crouching low in the grass, I watched as the bear came as close as fifty feet from me, reaching that fork in the trail and veering off, strolling away from me.

I learned two self-defense lessons that day. One, listen to your intuition. And two, learn from any source possible and be prepared. You don't have to face confrontation to learn about self-defense. When was the last time you felt your sixth sense attempting to warn you? Trust your instincts. Listen to them. It just may save your life.

Chapter 35

Do You Know What to Do When Facing a Confrontation?

The classroom fell silent. The head instructor was putting students on the spot again. He had this habit of posing self-defense scenarios then asking you about them. Many times you would think you've heard this scenario before, but he would change the details to keep you on your toes. On this particular day, the student standing immediately to my right was given the following scenario.

Your dog was sick and you just dropped him off at the vet. You still don't know what's wrong with him. This upsets you. You're quite mentally distracted and didn't notice the person coming in to the gas station as you were walking out. You accidentally brush shoulders with the guy. He clearly sees this as aggression, and turns around to confront you. The man rushes in between you and your car in a confrontational manner and is now blocking your access to your vehicle. What do you do?

It was at this point that the student beside me started saying something along the lines of "I ask the guy what his problem is." To which the instructor asks, "So you say to him, 'What's your (expletive) problem?' in a very negative and aggressive tone."

The lesson becomes very clear. This is not the correct way to neutralize the situation.

Why didn't you just walk away in the first place? Do you really need this hassle?

It becomes clear indeed, that a well thought out self-defense strategy includes learning specific dialogue to help the student avoid confrontation in the best way possible and further insulate them if the situation becomes violent. Always simply walk away if possible. If the situation makes it difficult to walk away, you must turn it into a self-defense situation.

Learn the following dialogue.

1. "Is there a problem?"
2. "Is there something I can help you with?" or "How does it involve me?"
3. "I don't want any trouble."

There is no need to repeat the last statement over and over again. If the aggressor is close, you have your hands up with your palms open. This gives off a non-violent quality for anyone who may be witnessing this event from a distance. Yet the fact is that you are actually in your fighting stance. The only difference is that your palms are open. For the potential witnesses who can hear what is going on, you have clearly stated that you don't want any trouble.

If he attacks you, you will be defending yourself and will be justified in using as much force as needed to stop the attack and prevent it from continuing. What is your plan?

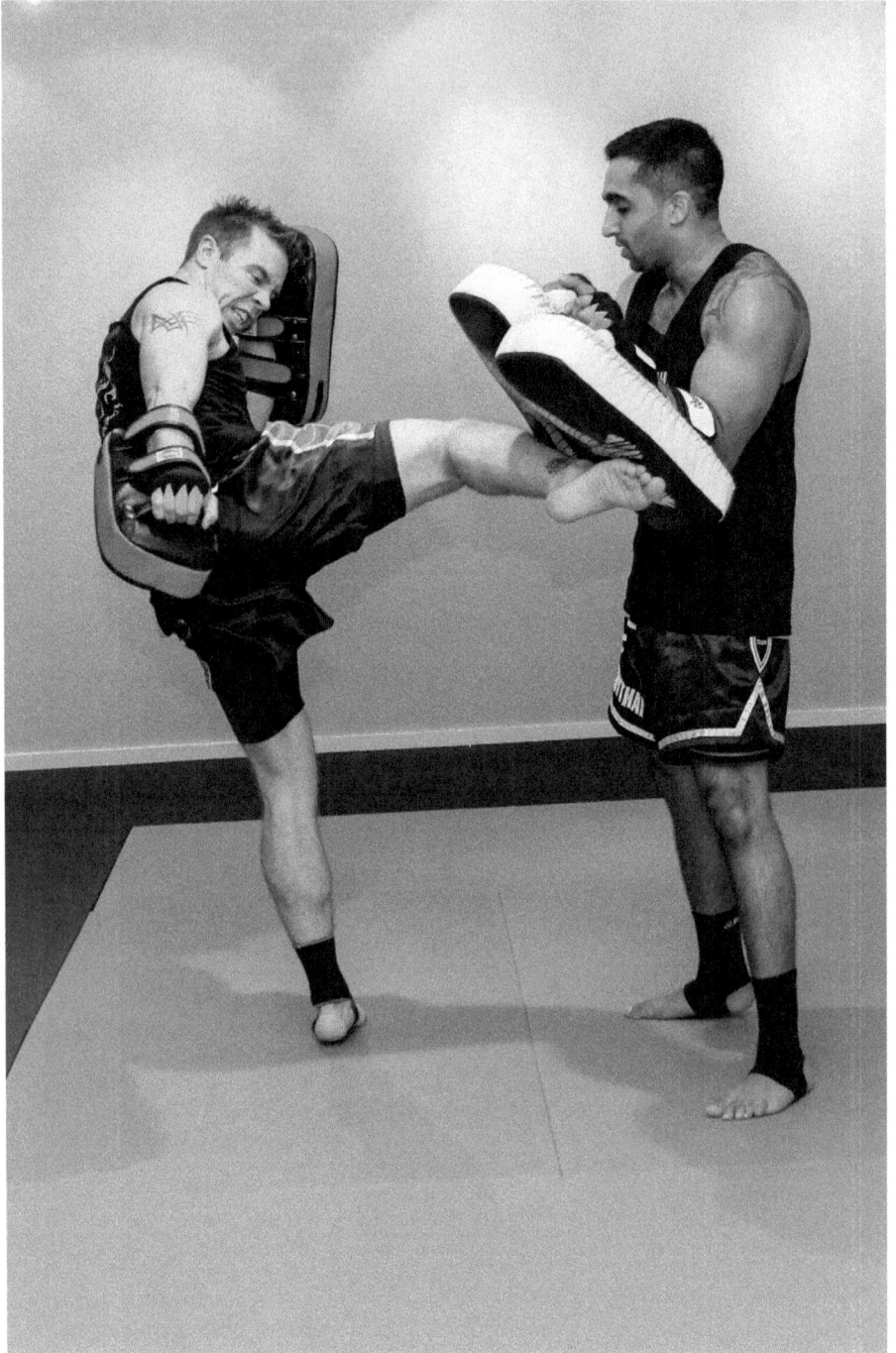

Chapter 36
What Is Your Martial Philosophy?

Serious injury can result from a violent confrontation. Therefore, the serious student of the martial arts adopts a mindset and a lifestyle of non-violence. We do everything possible to avoid a violent, physical confrontation for many reasons.

The reasons should be obvious.

- **The results can be catastrophic.** I have a file folder filled with news articles I have clipped over the years where a very small fight, a seemingly insignificant altercation, resulted in accidental death. A random tripping and landing badly on the concrete and one person is dead and the other's life is changed forever. I knew a person in elementary school who was involved in a school-yard fight. He beat the other child so bad that the other child was never the same and spoke a little slower. What an incredibly sad story. Do you want this on your conscience?
- **It's not necessary.** If you have trained for a long period of time, the chances are great that you are going to win the fight anyway. You are a trained individual, after all, so this fight is pointless.
- **You have nothing to prove.** After all the time and effort you have put in, your friends know you can defend yourself.

You know it as well. You don't need this fight to boost your ego.

- **It is philosophically degrading to become embroiled in physical conflict**, as it goes against your pre-determined rules of conduct, I hope. The fact is that becoming involved in a fight means that all other methods of avoidance have failed.
- **You don't have to prove anything to this person in front of you.** You'll probably never see them again. What do you care what some stranger thinks of you?
- **What legal challenges will you avoid by not fighting?**
- **There are other reasons as well.**

After a few years of training, you amass an arsenal of devastatingly effective techniques. Certain responsibility comes with this knowledge, and the serious martial artist knows this. The serious martial artist first chooses to avoid the violence.

Having a well established set of rules or your own "rules of engagement" established ahead of time will go a long way to make the decision-making much easier during the high stress of a potentially violent situation. Of course, when you have no choice and are forced into action, you hit as hard as you can and use 100% commitment until it is no longer needed. Your philosophy guides you. What is your philosophy?

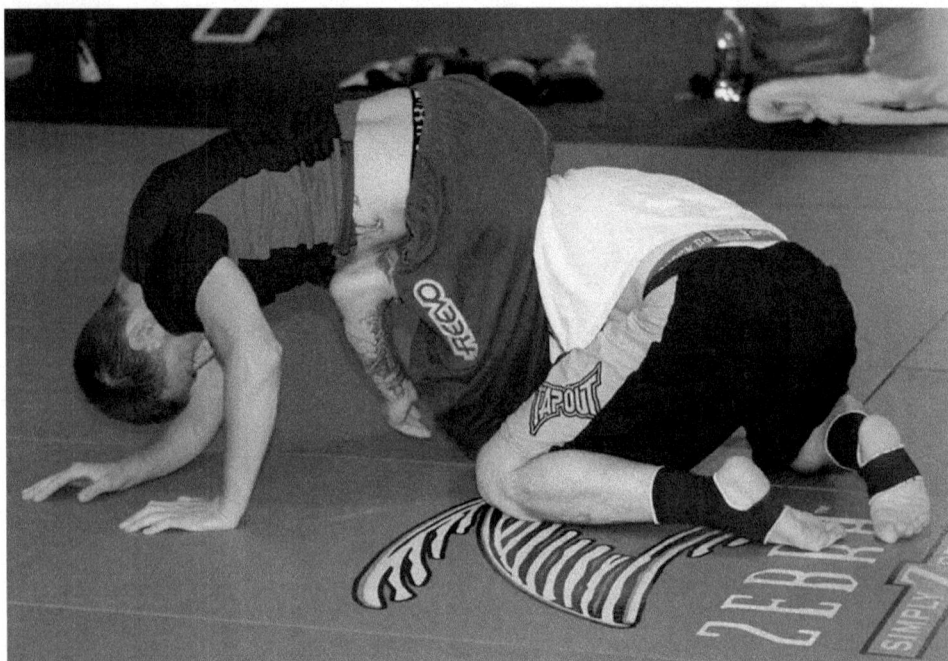

Chapter 37

The One Success Principle to Guide You to Black Belt Status and the Best Way to Attain It

"I don't have talent, I have tenacity."
— *Henry Rollins*

"I would rather go to the BBQ early and socialize a bit longer than hit the dojo for the evening class," you think to yourself. "Besides, there are always fewer students on Friday evenings anyway. And I am still sore from Wednesday's wicked workout."

Have you been trapped in this mindset before? Literally talking yourself out of attending class with one lame excuse or another? Chances are you have. And for those students who have kept at their training long enough to achieve black belt, they have had those same feelings as well. They are normal human beings just like you, but what kept them coming back for more? What caused them to continually show up to training over and over again until that highly sought after, highly coveted black belt finally found itself wrapped firmly around their waists? In a word, it is perseverance.

A worthwhile goal is not something that you will achieve in a short period of time. Bruce Lee must have been of this mindset when he said, "Do not pray for an easy life, pray for the strength to endure a difficult one." The goal of attaining black belt in any art is a tremendous goal that many refer to as a life-goal because of the perseverance and tenacity one must possess in order to see it through to fruition.

The best method in developing your tenacious perseverance is what I call "make a promise, keep a promise." The moment you find your training slipping, make a promise to yourself and keep it. Start out small, and make sure that no matter what happens, you will do what you said you would do. This one seemingly simple yet powerful technique will get you back on track. The key is to build on your success. As mentioned in a previous chapter, your habit will solidify in 30 days, so keep at it. This is such a powerful tool that you can use today, right now.

Make a promise, keep a promise.

Has your training frequency slowed down to a point where you barely attend class? Has your fitness routine slipped dramatically? When I mention above to start small, actually start small. Promise yourself that, no matter what happens, you will perform even just ten push ups, ten sit ups and ten squats today. It's not much and you can do it in minutes. But the fact that you kept your word to yourself will be amazing. You are in control now. Build on this. Promise yourself something slightly bigger tomorrow, and even bigger the next day. Confidence returns and, before you know it, you are back on track.

One powerful benefit of this is the following progression. The promise is small to begin with, so it's easy to take that little bit of action. But once you are actually moving, once you have overcome the initial inertia, you feel a tidal wave of motivation pour over you and you yearn so badly for the days when you experienced the results of your past perseverance that it snaps you back to discipline almost as if automatically!

Ordinary people attain extraordinary results when they have perseverance. Perseverance in the martial arts is absolutely mandatory in order to attain black belt. It is what separates the serious students from the rest. Learn from the above suggestions and the wisdom of Bruce, and you too will achieve your highest self. You too will wear that black belt. What is your best tip to help yourself persevere?

Chapter 38
Different Strokes

Some people think of the martial arts as a fun leisure activity, an amusing thing to do to pass the time. Of course, this is fine. Different strokes for different folks, right? Not everything you do needs to be deadly serious. We all need to unplug and kick our feet up from time to time. But martial arts is a life skill. It's a necessity in the world we find ourselves in.

If you approach training in the martial arts with a serious purpose, a few things must be considered. You must remember its history and why the martial arts developed in the first place. I should point out that I'm not talking about putting your kids into the martial arts. You need to consider an art or style that trains all ranges of combat and teaches you the mental aspects as well. There are many styles that fit the bill but traditional Ju-Jitsu or arts like it fit best.

The thug in the streets knows no rules to follow.

Traditional Ju-Jitsu usually trains all the ranges. It does not limit what the teachers teach simply because a technique may violate a rule in the ring during a competition. Styles that focus on just ground fighting only don't work at all if you have to defend yourself against multiple attackers. However, there are styles of Brazilian Ju-Jitsu, like the Carlson Gracie system for instance, that teach a well-balanced system, so don't read that I am bashing Brazilian Ju-Jitsu.

OF course there are many styles of Ju-Jitsu that focus on readying the students to win at the next competition. Training for or involving yourself in competition is not a bad thing. But if that is your only focus and you don't discuss self-defense scenarios, move on. If your goal is to prepare yourself against violent confrontation, train at a club that prepares you in all aspects of the conflict. This is the kind of club that teaches you to appreciate all the aspects of a violent confrontation, such as your stress response and how to deal with it. Learning at a club like this will instill in you the skills needed to face that confrontation with the appropriate responses.

If you're just starting out, realize that it will take up to six months to get a solid grasp of the fundamentals. You're not going to pick it up in a few easy lessons or in a weekend self-defense course. It is a bit more involved than that.

Chapter 39

A Lesson from the Master

The training session was over and we were inside Tom's house. While sitting on the couch discussing our training, Tom picked up a round heavy metal ball. This thing looked like a cannonball and weighed approximately 30 pounds. He didn't even seem to pay attention to the fact that he had picked it up and started performing arm curls, wrist curls and presses straight into the air as his conversation did not skip a beat.

I asked him about this and he shared a piece of knowledge he learned from Paul Vunak, who learned it from Danny Inosanto. Of course, Danny Inosanto is renowned for training directly with Bruce Lee. He is an authority in Jeet Kune Do and the Filipino martial arts, including Escrima and Silat. The piece of knowledge was that Bruce Lee was **"always training."** He always had his mind in his art and never missed an opportunity to train some aspect of it.

"Knowing is not enough, we must apply. Willing is not enough, we must do." - Bruce Lee

This knowledge is great, but how do I apply it? I attended a JKD seminar just after my time with Paul and Tom. A large portion of the seminar was devoted to the eye-jab tactic. Every possible way of training it was covered. In one particular instance, our instructor took some chalk and drew a set of eyes on our focus mitts. We then moved around with our partners as if fighting. When the focus mitt was held still, you had to strike the eyes with 100% accuracy. There was great emphasis on the accuracy factor.

I wanted to develop the skill of accuracy. So applying the knowledge about always training, I put up small, inconspicuous sets of "eyes" around my place of employment. Little tiny stickers set at eye level served my purpose well. As I walked by, when no one was looking, of course, I would reach out, and make the lightest contact to the target with 100% accuracy. I did this many times a day, every day. I was always training. As silly as this may sound, a few weeks later while instructing class, I was able to demonstrate this technique with a great deal of accuracy. It really worked!

What is a martial skill that you want to develop? How can you work aspects of it into your day, and throughout the day? Even mental faculties devoted towards visualizing your excellent performance will bring you closer to you goals. Your training isn't always physical. How can you be always training?

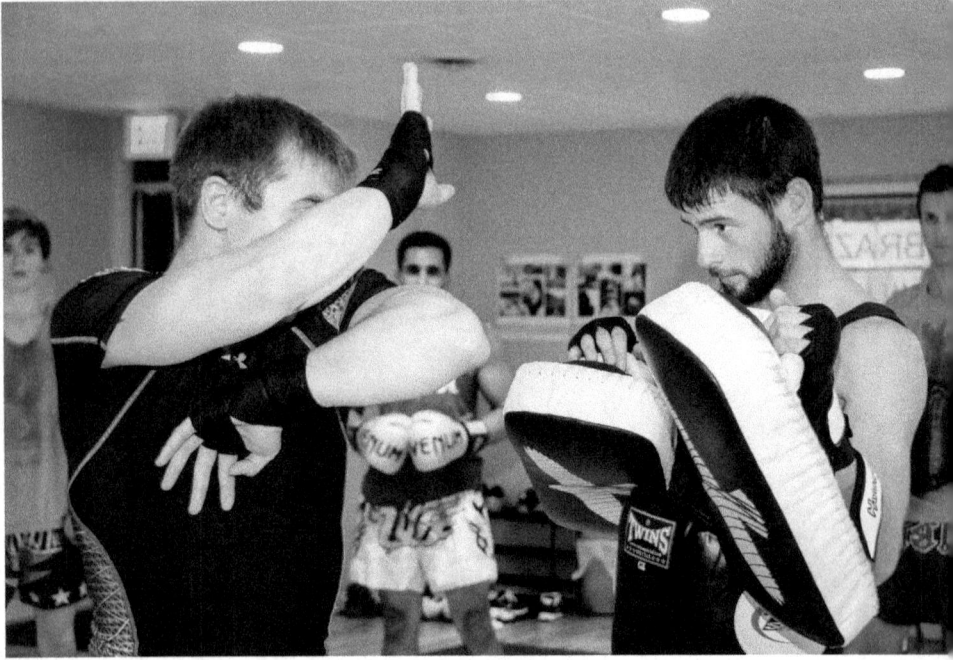

Chapter 40

7 Tried and True Methods to Stick With the Plan 'til You Reach Your First Dan

It can be easy to assume that the martial artist who has great skill, great timing, great ability and grace is simply talented. It's nice for us "regular" people to believe such things because it gives us a convenient excuse. It's not unlike the out-of-shape individual who suggests you are in good shape simply because you have "good genetics". Well, the excuse is fine for those without the experience to recognize the trap.

This thinking is a weak attempt to justify why we don't have to try so hard. It's convenient, I suppose, but not to the modern samurai. Not to someone who is serious about being all he can be with his personal martial pursuits. To these people, I offer seven ways to improve your discipline to ensure you achieve your goal, whether that is achieving black belt or any other goal.

Simply by upping your discipline, you can train more. And when a martial artist of 'ordinary talent' trains hard and regularly, he can easily outshine the more naturally-gifted individual who only trains halfheartedly. So let's get disciplined and even out the score.

The following tips will help you achieve your martial goals.

1. **"I don't feel like it."** A coach of mine recently said to me, "Not wanting to do something is never a good reason not to do it." This is true. Our goals are long-term, so use Nike's advice and 'just do it.'

2. **Never negotiate.** We have evolved to avoid physical exertion once our immediate needs are met. Recognize that although our nature is one to conserve energy, this is no longer required to survive. The moment your internal voice pops up to suggest you do anything other than start your martial arts training, shut it down immediately. The longer you listen to alternatives to your training plan, the more inertia builds up.

3. **Ignore the inessential.** Always evaluate what you devote your time to. Ask yourself, "Is this activity that I am about to do bringing me closer or farther away from my goals?" Act accordingly.

4. **Eliminate excuses.** I could write an entire chapter on the lies we tell ourselves. Simply being truly honest with yourself is the best gift you can give yourself. Examine the story you tell yourself. Did you really not have the time or did something else simply hold a higher priority to you? This will liberate you. I promise.

5. **Use external accountability.** An upcoming belt test is great. It gives you reason beyond yourself to train harder. If you don't have something beyond yourself, make a training goal and share it with as many people as you can. You don't want to let them down, do you? This will provide needed external accountability.

6. **Don't listen to anyone who doesn't have your best interest at heart.** These people really don't matter. What benefit to you is there in allowing a negative person to influence your mood? Use this negativity as fuel to your training fire.

7. **Always be a finisher.** I am not talking about a self-defense sequence this time. If something is worth starting, make

sure that you finish it. What you think about you bring about, so focus on how great you'll feel finally wearing your well-earned black belt.

The goal of achieving black belt is an admirable one. Use the techniques above to aid you in staying the course and achieving your martial dreams. What is your best tip or practice in maintaining training discipline?

Chapter 41

Put the Act Back In Distraction

"I was walking to my car and he just came out of nowhere. He grabbed me and assaulted me."

How many times have you heard the story of the lady that was walking down the street and, out of nowhere, she is attacked? Could this have been avoided? When you spend any amount of time reading the accounts of the victims of assault, a common theme emerges. This common theme is one of being unaware. The victim was unaware that a threat was present. There are potentially many reasons for this but one of the biggest contributing factors is the fact that they weren't paying attention to the warning signs of the potential for danger. They simply weren't paying attention because they were distracted.

In a previous chapter, I told a story about a pair of pick-pockets who attempted to distract me and a friend while we were on vacation. This is an example of a deliberate external distraction directed at you by a potential foe. The kind of distraction we're focusing on today is much worse. It is one that we allow. It occurs when we get complacent and assuming. This is what criminals look for. This is where we unintentionally allow ourselves to be an easy victim. This is unacceptable to the modern samurai.

Observe the scenarios below and remind yourself where you need to be more vigilant.

Distraction: A major contributor to the circumstances leading to victimization.

- The victim was busy looking in her purse for her car keys and didn't notice the mugger walking swiftly towards her.
- The victim was being deliberately distracted by an accomplice as he was struck from behind.
- The victim was busy on her phone and didn't notice the attacker following her into the park.
- The victim was caught up in the ordinary routine and was virtually on auto-pilot, not paying attention.
- The victim was mentally occupied with thoughts on work or the daily minutia.

Learn from the mistakes of others. A coach told me once that an intelligent person learns from their mistakes while a genius learns from the mistakes of others. Yes, experience is a great teacher, but some lessons are best learned without enduring the consequences of inattention. In fact, some of the consequences of inattention are deathly dire and can only be learned from examining the mistakes others have made.

For the next few days, check in on yourself frequently. Are you fully aware of your surroundings or are you distracted?

Photo Contributed by Author

Chapter 42
How Is Your Martial Attitude?

When you hear about the spirit of the samurai, you may have conjured up an image of an Asian guy. Perhaps he is wearing a mask, like a ninja, and you can only see his eyes. His confident gaze and self-assured stride speak volumes. He is magnetic and capable. It is his projected self-confidence that portrays the attitude of self-reliance and being self-assured.

So when you think about attitude in everyday martial arts, you know that it plays an important role. An important role? I am suggesting that proper attitude is critical.

Having the right attitude has a positive impact in so many areas in life and it has no different effect in training martial arts. It helps you persist when others stop showing up. It helps see you to your next belt test. And it certainly plays a role in a student getting to black belt in any school I've ever trained at.

Just the atmosphere of a club filled with students possessing the right attitude is a great place to train. Less ego and more honest help and input for the learning student. When your training partner is trying a move on you and he doesn't quite apply it correctly, do you stop him and allow him to get the correct position so he learns the technique correctly today? (Good attitude) Or do you let him continue, struggling because you don't want him to have another effective technique to use on you during sparring practice? (Bad attitude)

In many clubs, having and displaying the right attitude is a requirement before even being considered for promotion to the higher rankings. Can you imagine someone having a black belt in your club who had a terrible attitude? This person would not be a very good ambassador to the club. He would lower the regard of all the black belts in the club.

I remember introducing myself to a woman one time. When she found out that I was a senior-ranked belt at a particular school, she asked if I was one of "those guys". "Those guys?" I asked her. She went on to explain about a negative experience she had at the hands of one of the senior members of the club. Guilt by association is alive and well and will bring down a club's reputation if a bad apple is allowed to move up in the ranks. This particular fellow ended up being asked to take a hiatus from the club. He went on to open his own school. Best of luck to him.

"Choose the positive. You have a choice. You are the master of your attitude. Choose the positive, the constructive. Optimism is a faith that leads to success." ~ Bruce Lee

Photo Contributed by Author

Chapter 43
The Cornered Leopard Yawns

Have you ever observed a lion or other large cat about to engage in some form of territorial or mating dispute? Of course, you most likely watched it on the nature channel but even observing a domestic house cat just before it attacks its sister in a fun game of 'cat tackle' can reveal some very interesting strategies and tactics. Often times, it looks away and feigns disinterest the very moment before it leaps. The cornered leopard yawns.

There are other things nature provides, like adrenalin. Learning its effects and how to anticipate them and use them will provide you with an edge. If you find yourself forced into a physical altercation, it does you no good to give into the fear. When you are suddenly attacked; when you are forced to defend yourself, certain physiological changes take place in your body. The more you realize and understand this, the better off you'll be.

So just as the "cornered leopard yawns" when facing confrontation, so to should you not give your potential attacker any clues to your real intent. Do not cower, or show that you are afraid and that you definitely do not want to be attacked. Yes your adrenalin will be pumping, but just know, that when attacked, you will transform instantly from a yawning/uninterested leopard, unleashing all your might, and fury and destroy your assailant.

As covered in a previous chapter, your heart rate rises. This is one of the first things that happens as that adrenalin dump occurs to aid in your **fight or flight response**. Your vision can reduce to tunnel vision and your palms can start to sweat. You'll breathe faster or shallower, and remembering to breath slow and deep can help you maintain your focus. The excess adrenalin can cause you to shake a bit as well.

The biggest takeaway I want you to get here is not to be afraid of the fact that your body is experiencing this adrenaline dump. Be afraid? Gosh no! Understand that this adrenalin is your friend, a potential best friend if you understand it and use it.

If you can run away, you will be able to run fast and far with this adrenalin. But if you need to fight, which is what we're talking about here, that adrenalin is your best friend. Channel it and understand that people with adrenalin dumps can perform superhuman feats. How many times have you heard about the mother in a car crash lifting up a vehicle to save her child? That skinny woman lifting incredible amounts of weight while under an immense adrenalin dump is a perfect example of this.

When the bully looks at the kid and laughs with his friends, pointing out the fact that you are shaking, "Look at him, he's so scared. He's shaking like a leaf!" This bully does not realize that he's just done you a favor. He has given you the potential of superhuman strength, literally. When you learn to harness this gift and work with it, you will be able to react faster, hit harder and focus 100% on destroying the threat in front of you, and making it home safe.

Chapter 44
Self-Defense: Your Global Approach

The first time I heard of the martial arts having a global approach was from Dr. Serge LaFlamme. I am honored to be his student. This man has dedicated his life to the martial pursuits and his resume speaks volumes. He was referring, of course, to the style of Sogo-Ryu Ju-Jitsu, of which he is the founder.

Most people, when they hear the words self-defense, conjure up images in their heads of students learning a move to stop a punch or a kick. But not the serious student of the martial arts. The serious student, or the modern samurai, understands that self-defense occurs all the time. It is all-pervasive. It is present during your morning commute, all the way up to and even including while you sleep at night in your bed at home. Protecting yourself and your family at home is just as important as your physical tactics.

"So I have to be on guard all the time? I want to relax when I get home." I do hear these queries and quickly mention that no, you don't have to be on guard all the time, not if you take the necessary precautions ahead of time. Fortify your home to lessen the chance of an intruder forcing you to thrash them. Being somewhat passionate about personal protection and self-reliance, I have taken some locksmiths courses. I was shocked at how easily most inexpensive locks can be opened by anyone willing to take the time to watch a few Youtube videos.

Unless you are being targeted specifically, the sad truth is that all you have to do to protect your home is make it a little less accessible than your neighbor's home. Criminals want the most for the least. If they can steal from your neighbor's home easier than yours and with less noise, they won't bother you. They look for easy opportunities, not hassles.

A crime of opportunity.

So compare your home to your neighborhood homes. How does yours compare? Would your home provide opportunity or adversity to the opportunistic jerk that would violate your sanctuary?

Consider the following.

1. Does your home have large shrubs or bushes by the windows to allow a thief cover while they work on the lock or jimmy the window?
2. Does it have large shrubs or other cover where a criminal can hide behind to work on your door lock, or even ambush you as you unlock your door at night?
3. Do you have trees beside the walls, giving the tree-climbing intruder an advantage?
4. Are you silly enough to store ladders or other entry tools outside your home in unlocked sheds? (I have a neighbor directly behind my house who has no less than three ladders stored on the outside of his house. Hope his upper floor windows are locked!)
5. How about a home security system or at least some decals or signage? I may not pay the local security monitoring company monthly, but I feel I am being nice to them by printing out their logo and putting it in a window on each side of my home.
6. Consider a dog.
7. Do you have a light or two set with timers, and maybe even a radio?

8. Do you have external motion-activated lighting?

9. Do you have bars on all lower windows or at least the ones in the backyard?

There are certainly more things to consider, but this is a good start. Of course, as a modern samurai, your attitude would not be one of "let them get my neighbors, and not me." Talk to your neighbors. Be friendly. If you are a local instructor of the martial arts, print out this chapter or make your own flyer and inform your neighbors how they too can protect themselves and their property. Band together and watch out for suspicious activity in your neighborhood. This is the attitude of standing united. This is the attitude of the Modern Samurai.

Chapter 45
Are You A Modern Samurai?

"A goal is not always meant to be reached. It often serves simply as something to aim at." - Bruce Lee

Are you a career soldier? Or perhaps a peace officer? Maybe you're someone who long ago devoted a serious portion of your life to the martial pursuits? Do you have to be in one of these career paths or one similar to be considered a modern samurai?

You don't have to be a soldier who meditates daily and practices martial arts to be considered one. You may wear a suit and commute to work in your sports car or take public transit and still be the complete embodiment of the modern samurai. It doesn't matter whether you are white, black, male or female. No matter what you are, you can still qualify. And, of course, you don't have to be of Asian descent to fall into the category. Every time you bring your focus to the following question or one like it, you pass the litmus test.

What is the question? It is simply this: "Is what I am doing right now or plan to do immediately something a modern samurai would do?" Or phrased differently, "Is what I am doing or about to do bringing me closer or farther away from my idea of the modern samurai?"

If you make your goal to be following the path of the modern samurai, consider the wisdom of Bruce Lee. You don't have to reach it every day but you must aim at it. To error is human, so forgive yourself when you miss a training session. Don't beat yourself up. Beat up your heavy bag. Again, consider Bruce Lee's words: "Mistakes are always forgivable, if one has the courage to admit them."

Admit your mistakes, and move on.

I, too, sometimes find myself at odds with the ideals of how I would like to be living my life. Perhaps it is a health-destructive habit or some other distraction that causes me to miss a training session. At these moments, it is very important to ask yourself, "Is what I'm about to do bringing me closer to my ideals of the modern samurai or will it push me further away?" Let the answer guide you.

It's not about being the perfect model of the modern samurai that is important. It is embracing the struggle! Face your own personal demons and conquer them. Actively choose to change course the minute, no, the instant you find yourself straying off the righteous path you committed to long ago. That is the stuff that meaningful lives are made of. That is what makes you the modern samurai.

Connect with Us!

Now it is your turn. It's your time to join the ranks of the modern samurai. You can do so easily, and without cost by sending me an email to Al@ModernSamuraiSociety.com. Be sure to attach your martial picture and bio and you will soon see yourself up in the ranks of dedicated martial artists who rank from first-degree black belt all the way up to 10th degree. You will recognize some pretty big names who have all given me their express permission. They, too, like you, sent me their profiles which are proudly displayed in the members' area on the site.

If you have a trained any type of martial art for more than a couple of years, this site is for you. The Modern Samurai Society recognizes that serious martial artists share certain qualities or philosophy not just on the martial arts but also in how we conduct ourselves in everyday life. We strive towards continual self-improvement not just in our art of choice, but in every aspect of our existence that matters to us. In essence, we strive to attain the embodiment of the modern samurai.

Membership is free to those with a martial background. I encourage you to submit a picture and a bio to allow other members to know their fellow modern samurai. Feel free to include details of your own philosophy on the martial arts. If you are an instructor or run your own club, please submit a picture of your club and a short write-up containing any details you would like us to know; training schedule, location, upcoming events, and any other information pertaining to your club.

You'll also find detailed accounts of self defense in action and amazing instructional tips for the student as well as the instructor to aid you in every aspect of your journey. So please enjoy the content assembled for you and comment on the articles, adding your own wisdom that you have learned from your own martial journey. Remember, "**Standing united, we pack a punch!**"

About the Author

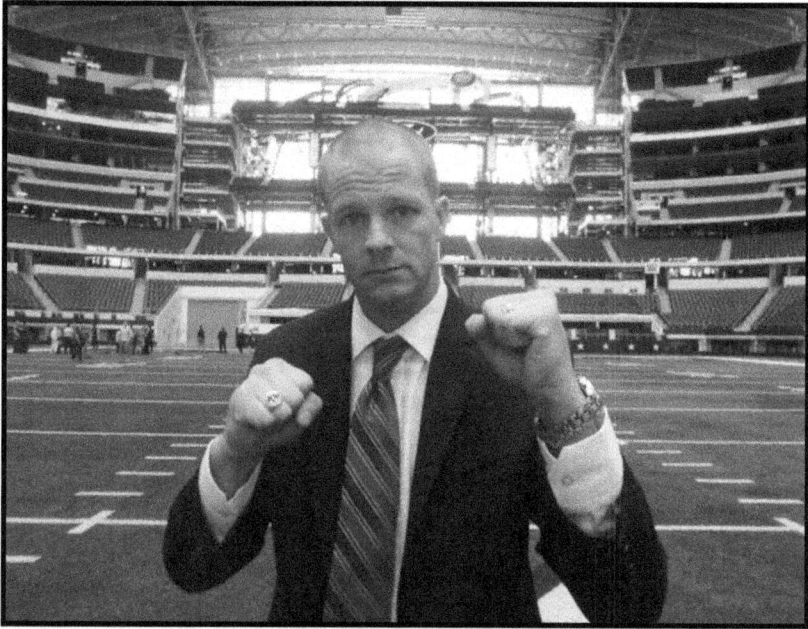

Al entered his first martial arts class at the tender of age of 11 in 1983. Since then, he has trained in five separate kinds of martial arts but focused on three styles, namely: traditional Karate (**Kempo** and **Chito Ryu**), **Jeet Kune Do** and traditional **Jiu-Jitsu** with a few years of **Brazilian Jujitsu** thrown in just for fun.

Al has found tremendous value in holding a valid security license and working part-time in the security field, with his primary function in event security at concerts and as a bouncer and bodyguard for VIP clients. No matter how many times you practice a hook punch defense in the dojo, the experience of engaging in a real physical altercation is priceless.

Being passionate about the martial arts and fitness, Al vowed to record every lesson, every tip and every training tool about the martial arts and personal protection. These you can find at ModernSamuraiSociety.com, where you can subscribe to the newsletter and Al's "Number 1, No-Fail Self Defense Technique."

About the Photographer

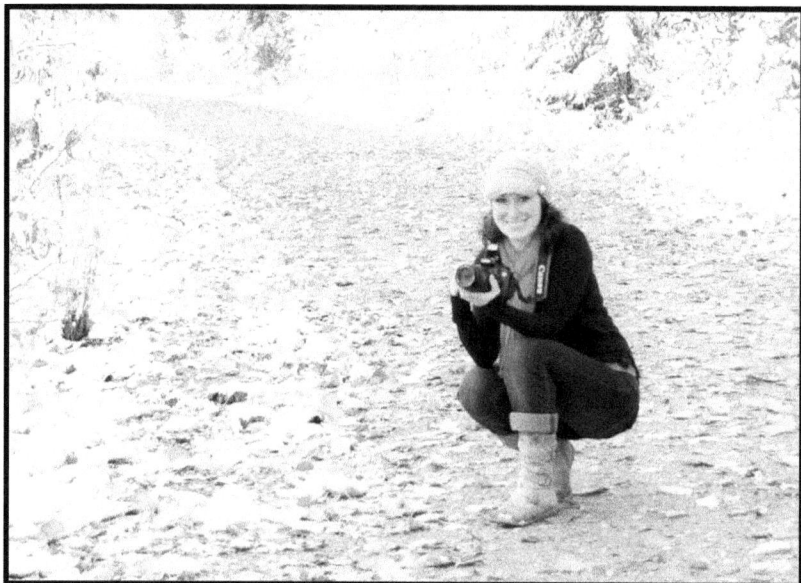

Kasey Lane Howery was born and raised in British Columbia's Okanagan valley. Her passion for telling stories through pictures led to a career in photography that includes families, engagements and weddings. You can contact her through Facebook.com/KaseyLanePhotography

www.ingramcontent.com/pod-product-compliance
Lightning Source LLC
LaVergne TN
LVHW051511080426
835509LV00017B/2018